Mike!
Wall Street's Mayor

To Joan

Mike!
Wall Street's Mayor

Neil Fabricant

Illustrations by Keith Seidel

HACKS & FLACKS PRESS
NEW YORK, NEW YORK

Mike! Wall Street's Mayor
Text © Copyright 2012 Neil Fabricant
Illustrations © Copyright 2012 Keith Seidel
Cover design by Jay Van Buren (Early-Adopter.com)

First Edition
ISBN: 978-0-9849111-1-0

Library of Congress Control Number: 2011945338

Published by:

    Hacks & Flacks Press
    a Division of Bloomberg Watch Inc.
    New York, NY 10013

www.WallStreetsMayor.com

Typeset in the UK by Sally Lansdell (editexpert.350.com)
Printed in the United States of America

Contents

We must make our choice. We may have democracy, or we may have wealth concentrated in the hands of a few, but we can't have both.
—United States Supreme Court Justice Louis D. Brandeis

My Perspective

I'm a born-and-raised New Yorker. I've lived here all my life. Michael Bloomberg came from somewhere else, made a fortune on Wall Street, and decided to buy City Hall and whichever of New York's political and civil institutions were for sale—which turned out to be most of them. From its inception, his mayoralty has been rooted in the idea that the city is a business and he is its CEO.

In a closed-to-the-press talk he gave to a group of businessmen on January 7, 2003, Mike said, "If New York City is a business, it isn't Wal-Mart—it isn't trying to be the lowest-priced product in the market. It's a high-end product, maybe even a luxury product."[1]

Attracting and servicing high-value businesses and those who can afford to live and work here has always been the plan. That's what explains the proliferation of luxury condominiums, the erosion of the city's affordable housing, the small businesses driven out in favor of large retail chains, the high-end commercial and office space, and the billion-dollar sports stadiums subsidized by New Yorkers who already live here and can't afford to live in the condominiums, dine in the upscale restaurants, or attend the stadiums they helped pay for. Maybe the starkest example of this misguided vision is the demise of St. Vincent's in Greenwich Village. The 758-bed hospital that served the community for more than 150 years will be replaced by 450 luxury condominiums. The rich will always have top-notch health care. In Mike's World, that's progress.

Despite the relentless self-promotion regarding his fiscal and management skills, when this mayor leaves office we will be looking at large budget deficits as far as the eye can see.[2] The city's outstanding debt has passed $100 billion, an increase of 83 percent since 2002, the year he took office. Debt service is projected to be 10 percent of the city's expense budget by 2015.[3]

After almost twelve years under his control, our public schools are by far the most policed and remain among the most segregated in the nation. He claims to have worked miracles, but by all credible measures our schools are failing as badly as ever. He claims to be sympathetic to the poor and working hard for the middle class, but the city's wealth and income disparities are the most extreme we've ever known.[4] He says New York is a glitzy, happening place, but a shocking number of people are barely surviving:

- 3.1 million New Yorkers now live at or near the poverty line ($22,314 for a family of four).

- About 900,000 New Yorkers live in deep poverty, which is half of the federal poverty level; for a four-person family that means an income of little more than $10,500.
- 1,100,000 households pay at least half their income for rent. They have about $30 a week per family member for food, medical expenses, transportation, education, and anything else they need.[5]
- The city's average rent is more than 50 percent higher than the second most expensive city in the United States, San Francisco.
- If you earn $50,000 in Houston, you'd need at least $125,000 in New York to maintain the same lifestyle.[6]

Everything families need—rent, schooling, childcare, utility bills, groceries—has risen dramatically. The skyrocketing costs New Yorkers have experienced during the past decade aren't a law of nature; they are in substantial part the result of man-made policies—one man in particular: Michael Bloomberg, the city's richest man.

He rejects the notion that Wall Street created the financial wreckage, vehemently opposes higher taxes on the rich, and fights against stricter regulation of Wall Street. In his world, it was the 1977 Community Reinvestment Act, the business cycle, Congress, people who bought homes they couldn't afford, Freddie Mac, and so forth that brought the country to its knees. Sure, some Wall Street firms made "mistakes," but the stockholders and bondholders paid for them so let's move on.

◄o►

New York's 58 billionaires and countless multimillionaires, who travel the city streets in chauffeured limousines behind tinted windows, hail Bloomberg as the *Best Mayor Ever*. Black kids walking in their own neighborhoods better be carrying identification and even if they are, they just might be slammed up against a wall, humiliated, searched, and abused in ways big and small. The mayor and his police chief deny it, but cops have arrest quotas and the places they go to fill them are poor neighborhoods of color. Each year hundreds of thousands of young black and Hispanic males are illegally stopped, frisked, searched, and arrested ... because they're black and Hispanic ... in New York ... in 2012.

No, Bloomberg isn't entirely to blame. We'll always have rich people and poor people; crooked and brutal cops; racists and meretricious politicians; killer real estate operators and Wall Street hustlers wearing $5,000 suits who will rip your face off—but we've never had a mayor like this. Wall Street's war on America, its assault on the poor, on people of color, on working- and middle-class people, and its ownership of our political and civic institutions can be seen nowhere more clearly than right here in New York City—in City Hall. But many good people still don't see it.

◄o►

In his book *On Bullshit*, Dr. Harry G. Frankfurt, Princeton University philosophy professor emeritus, writes, "One of the most salient features of our culture is that there is so much bullshit. Everyone knows it, and most people think they can recognize it, but often they can't."[7]

You can't understand Michael Bloomberg without having Professor Frankfurt's caution in mind. And when you understand Michael Bloomberg—or "Mike," as his handlers prefer—you understand much of what's gone wrong with America. Not that understanding Mike is easy: his character, his ideology, and his methods have been obscured by a decade-long campaign of propaganda and payoffs. Even Howard Dean, a man I admire and respect, called him a great mayor. Dean wasn't paying attention.

The nearly $300 million that Bloomberg officially poured into his three campaigns has blown through any semblance of democratic elections, but that figure doesn't begin to tell the whole story. It doesn't count the influence of his "charitable" contributions, which rose from $100 million in 2000 to $235 million in 2008, much of it concentrated on New York's civic institutions. Nor does it include the vast sums of taxpayer dollars—our money—that he's awarded in contracts, grants, and subsidies to his supporters. Nor does it take into account the retinue of hacks and flacks on his private payroll and those on the city payroll who are paid to trumpet his accomplishments.

The Republican and Independence Party leaders who sold him their ballot lines and the union presidents, politicians, and clergymen who took his money and sang his praises have payrolls to meet, grants and government contracts they want, labor negotiations to worry about, and careers to advance. They have been indispensable in promoting his narrative: *Just Mike, the incorruptible, $1-a-year public servant who wants to give something back.* Their reasons for supporting him may have once been understandable, but that time is long past.

The mega-billionaire with his thumb in your citizen's eye isn't Boss Tweed. We won't find $50,000 in small bills stashed in his freezer. Mike is a buyer of political power, not a seller of political favor. Nonetheless, since becoming mayor his personal fortune has soared from an estimated $3–$4 billion to $18–$20 billion. His is a private company, and even the most skilled and motivated reporters have had trouble uncovering just how he's done it. But they've found some things that are included in this book.

I think about New York's mayor as Mark Twain thought about William Clark, who in his time was also one of the country's wealthiest men. Clark wanted to be a US senator. At the time, they were chosen by state legislatures. He bribed the Montana legislature to give him a Senate seat, and he sat in it from 1901 until 1907. His rationale? "I never bought a man who wasn't for sale."[8] Mark Twain said this about Clark:

> *He is as rotten a human being as can be found anywhere under the flag; he is a shame to the American nation, and no one has helped to send him to the Senate who did not know that his proper place was the penitentiary, with a ball and chain on his legs. To my mind he is the most disgusting creature that the republic has produced since Tweed's time.*

Tweed took bribes and ended up in jail. Clark was on the other side of the transactions and didn't. Mike won't go to jail either. "Corrupt" is not the same as "illegal." Its literal meaning is morally unsound or debased. But he's taken things further than Tweed or Clark dreamed of. Mike represents the transition from the super-rich influencing government to *being* the government.

His domination of the nation's financial and media capital is unprecedented. But when he pointed out that "I have my own army in the NYPD, which is the seventh biggest army in the world. I have my own State Department, much to Foggy Bottom's annoyance. We have the United Nations in New York, and so we have an entree into the diplomatic world that Washington does not have," what we heard was not pride but petulance that his leadership qualities hadn't propelled him to a spot on the national ticket—at least.

When he didn't get it, he overturned term limits. That's when all New Yorkers should have understood that his disdain for voters wasn't an aberration. It was Mike being Mike, the city's CEO. If we didn't like what he was doing, he said, we could "boo him at parades."

Before his first term began, I found myself in a four-year struggle as the head of a 3,500-person tenant association in a rent-regulated complex in Manhattan. Our landlord was making life hell for us. It was the 2001 mayoral election. We needed political help. Mike was the only politician who didn't need the real estate money; I urged tenants to support him.

I was naïve. I soon discovered that the notorious real estate predator, Laurence ("Call me Larry") Gluck, had an enthusiastic ally in Mike, the Affordable Housing Mayor. That struggle was my introduction to Mike and his administration, and it was the catalyst for this book. Thus there are two stories being told, that of Independence Plaza and that of Mike. Some who have read the early drafts suggested that they are different stories and don't belong in the same book. I think they're mistaken. What happened at Independence Plaza is the kind of story that—if it is told at all—gets filtered through public relations and political professionals and filtered again through the reporting and editorial conventions of the *New York Times* and other mainstream media. The distortions, omissions, and flat-out lies become the official history. And that, as we'll see in the reporting of the Independence Plaza story, is a story in itself.

◄◦►

I'm told too that unless I take a more nuanced approach, search for and write about the good things he's done, all the people and institutions he's supported, that my credibility will be diminished. I stipulate to those good things. I'm sure there are some. My intention has been not to write the definitive biography of one of the most important figures in the city's history. Historians will do that in due course. The purpose of this book is to point up some (by no means all) of the negative aspects of his character and career that aren't as widely known as they should be, and, by explaining why they aren't known, to reveal aspects of New York's insider political culture.

I have no "isms" to advance, no manifestos to proclaim, no theories of urban government to propound. I write from the perspective of someone who was once a political insider, an angle of vision that's hard to come by without suffering the blunted ethical sensibility that comes from being one. For years I headed a university-based research institute that was funded through contracts, foundation grants, and legislative appropriations. Before that, I had been a counsel to the Republican state senate majority leader.

The money I made and the benefits I enjoyed all came from insiders. When a group of foundations led by the Ford Foundation asked me to take over a magazine on New York government and politics that they had financed, I did it gladly. When it came to publishing everything I knew, I didn't. I even hired a couple of people at the research institute that I wouldn't have hired but for the fact that these same insiders asked me to do it. It's hard to unbundle self-interest from genuine feelings of friendship toward people who have helped you, but as with those who take Mike's money, there's always a rationale. Nobody wants to live an ignoble life.

There's also hypocrisy. When you've dined at the king's table and then throw the plate in his face from a safe distance, the charge is legitimately made. I worry about it. I can only say in mitigation that it wasn't until he went to prison that Teamster President Jimmy Hoffa became a passionate advocate for prison reform. And it wasn't until I experienced how Mike and a host of Democratic politicians dealt with people whose homes were at stake that I understood what it felt like to be an outsider.

I was fortunate to discover a brilliant cartoonist, Keith Seidel, whose images contribute so much to bringing Mike's story to life.

BOOK ONE

Call Me Mike!

—◀○▶—

Once integrity goes, the rest is a piece of cake.
J.R. Ewing

CHAPTER ONE

A Determined
Little Guy

Michael Bloomberg grew up in Medford, Massachusetts, a working-class town about an hour outside of Boston. He was one of the youngest Eagle Scouts ever. Sometimes he smoked and gambled with the townies. Mike was no pushover.

Early signs of the man we know emerged at Johns Hopkins, his undergraduate college. A young woman who went to the movies on a double date with Mike and a fraternity brother told this story to Joyce Purnick, a former *New York Times* reporter who produced an admiring biography of Mayor Bloomberg:

> We started to get in the line. He said, "Screw this." … He goes to the first person in the line, pushes twenty dollars at him, and said, "Get us four tickets." He got us four tickets and we walked in. That is the kind of chutzpah I'm talking about.[9]

Sticking with Yiddish, "chutzpah" didn't quite do it for the folks on line; maybe "putz."

In 1966, following four years at Johns Hopkins and two at Harvard Business School, Mike landed a job on Wall Street with Salomon Brothers & Hutzler. It was there that young Mike learned many of the salesman skills and the "us v. them" attitude that would serve him so well in his political career. He was the firm's first MBA.

Wall Street Salesman

Michael Lewis, author of the bestselling *Liar's Poker,* was a Salomon Brothers bond trader in the 1980s. He described how Salomon sold its customers worthless securities from its own proprietary account, a practice called "jamming." Tom Strauss, Salomon's president, told Lewis not to worry about it: "Customers have very short memories."[10]

If a salesman "could make millions of dollars come out of those phones," Lewis wrote, "he became that most revered of all species: a 'Big Swinging Dick.' A managing director would call and congratulate him, 'Hey, you Big Swinging Dick, way to be.'"[11]

In his memoir, Mike wistfully recalled his own Salomon days:

We could sell anything to anybody ... "It has a strong specialist behind it," I'd tell one buyer who might not have the slightest idea why the specialist mattered ... "The chart pattern looks like a breakout," Perry [Mike's closest friend] would declare for those who believed "the trend's my friend." I'd add, "Look at who the buyers and sellers have been," for the "misery loves company" crowd. Or, "You buy this and we'll help you sell that," we'd say, as if we wouldn't do either separately.[12]

Mike was a selling machine and years later he was still proud of it. "I was the fair-haired boy, the block trading superstar in the most visible department of the trendiest firm on the Street," he reminisced.

He asked John Gutfreund, Salomon's number two man (Gutfreund succeeded Billy Salomon as the firm's managing partner in 1979), to make him chief of staff—a gatekeeper between the boss and everybody else.

Gutfreund said no. Mike—with that endearing cut-to-the-front-of-the-line style and burning ambition—had made some important enemies. When the new partners list came out, he wasn't on it. Mike was humiliated. But a few months later, Billy Salomon called him in to his office to tell him he'd made partner. Finally! He'd be a Big Swinging Dick.

Billy Salomon didn't explain the delay, and Mike didn't ask. In his memoir Mike would later write, "He was, as I have become, a member of the 'never apologize, never explain' school of management." And so Mike joined some of our most egregious public figures, alumni of that same school.

Still, he was pissed off about being passed over the first time. The inner Mike was a slow-burning fire, but one day he would stoke it and show his enemies who they were dealing with.

In 1978, Mike was forced out of sales and into the computer department where he ran the firm's information systems. Two years later, as another firm was acquiring Salomon, the executive committee decided they had had enough of him. Gutfreund had to let him go. The firm gave him at least $10 million as his share of the partnership and sent him on his way. He was thirty-nine years old and had spent fifteen years at Salomon.

It was a lucky break. Mike wasn't at the firm when a major scandal prompted SEC chairman Dick Breeden to characterize Salomon as "rotten to the core." Gutfreund was forced to resign. Warren Buffett took over Salomon's chairmanship, saving it from prosecution and probable extinction.

Buffett didn't think much of Gutfreund. Billy Salomon called him a "disgrace."[13] Yet to this day Mike describes his former boss as "principled and honest."[14] We will meet many more of Mike's principled and honest friends as he moves from Wall Street to politics.

The Entrepreneur

Mike thought he'd join another Wall Street firm. But word had gotten around: Watch out for this guy. He'll eat your lunch and chew on your furniture. Nobody made him an offer.

If not stocks and bonds, what *could* he sell? Mike became very depressed. What to do, what to do? Mike enjoyed a little pot now and then so maybe one day he lit up a joint and the idea that changed his life came to him in a flash.

The similarities to the career of William Clark, the millionaire who never bought a man who wasn't for sale, are uncanny. During the California Gold Rush, Clark, a miner himself, sold pickaxes, underwear, food, and all the other stuff the miners needed. That's how he got so rich.

If Mike couldn't be a Wall Street trader, he'd sell traders the financial data they needed—on terminals right on their desks. As with Clark, his timing was perfect. Financial deregulation and globalization were just getting started. Home and car loans were being packaged and sold as securities; Wall Street was about to blow up.

Mike hired some software designers and financial analysts, and they all worked very hard to develop the machine that has made it so much easier for Wall Street to price and sell those collateralized debt obligations, derivatives, credit default swaps, and all the wonderful inventions of modern finance by which Wall Street bankers and their hired help in Washington have looted the country. ("Hired help" may seem glib, but Illinois Senator Richard Durbin noted that even after they took the country down, "the banks … are still the most powerful lobby on Capitol Hill. And they frankly own the place."[15])

◄o►

Merrill Lynch gave the new company, then known as Innovative Market Systems, its first big contract and became a 30 percent shareholder. Mike ran the company and did all the selling. Sometimes he even hooked up the terminals. He was never afraid to get his hands dirty.

The company grew and grew and grew. Mike was a tireless worker, and he knew how to sell to Wall Street's Big Swinging Dicks. He hired young, smart, pretty women. Known on the Street as "Bloomberg Women," the dress code was short skirts and "fuck me" shoes. Mike inspired them with his legendary wit. Reportedly, in one of his more famous pep talks about his new machine, he announced that "It will do everything, including give you a blow job. I guess that puts a lot of you girls out of business."[16] Sure, some women resented that kind of thing. But Mike paid well and didn't take criticism kindly. High-paying jobs for women on Wall Street were scarce.

By 1992 he had made Forbes' list of the 400 richest Americans. He took to strutting around his office, proclaiming his business philosophy, talking dirty to the women who worked for him, and just having a little fun.

One day, a female employee presented him with a 32-page, leather-bound booklet titled "The Portable Bloomberg: The Wit and Wisdom of Michael Bloomberg." It hasn't been widely distributed.

Here are some of Mike's key business principles and a few of his many insights on human nature:

Okay, it's not Ben Franklin's *Poor Richard's Almanac*, but Mike hadn't yet become the statesman he is today.

Not so surprisingly, a number of employees brought lawsuits charging sexual harassment. In one case, Mike's pre-trial deposition was sealed and the case was settled, reportedly for a high six-figure amount. How much money? The women who got cash settlements aren't talking. They signed confidentiality agreements. It was a lot, though.

Later, when he became a candidate and reporters asked him about the sexual harassment charges, Mike said they weren't true; whatever he may have said or done to offend those women was just "Borscht Belt humor."

New York magazine columnist Michael Wolff, who searched the court filings on three harassment charges, wrote that the *New York Times* had the documents but that the *Times* Metro editor wouldn't return his phone calls to discuss the issue.

Wolff did speak to the former Bloomberg employee who compiled "Wit and Wisdom." She confirmed its authenticity and assured him that the quotes were verbatim and that there was much more that didn't make it into the book. Wolff reported that the woman had been "muzzled by Bloomberg's attorneys, Willkie Farr & Gallagher, who had accused her of violating her confidentiality agreement with Bloomberg."

Mike took a lie detector test with the same polygraph expert used by Jeffrey Skilling, the former Enron president. The expert said that both men passed the test. Skilling released the results and went to jail. Mike refused to release them, had the pre-trial depositions sealed, the women sworn to secrecy, and is serving his third term as mayor. There's a lesson there but I'm not sure what it is.

Mike Comes Out

By 1995 he was jetting to his mansions around the world and helicoptering to his estate in Westchester and to the Hamptons. When not airborne, he was driven by limousine. His feet hardly ever touched the ground. He had all the sex he could handle and all the money he'd ever need. He explained to a London reporter: "I am a single, straight billionaire in Manhattan. It's like a wet dream."

Life was good. There was just one thing: except for the financial press, newspapers rarely wrote about him. People didn't know who he was. That made him so spitting mad, he could barely conceal the inner Mike.

Maybe they don't know Innovative Market Systems is really me, he thought.

So he changed the company name to Bloomberg LP and put it on everything he owned.

Even with the name change and thousands of his desktop terminals installed all over the world—yes, they are called *Bloombergs*—the public still didn't know who he was. *What the hell do I have to do to get some recognition?*

Maybe, just maybe … Hmmm, I better sleep on that one. And he did.

The next morning, he called his mother, whose advice he often sought. "Michael," she said, "What do you know about politics? Maybe you won't even like it. Start small; maybe try mayor first."

She was right! He'd be mayor of New York and see if he liked it. He enlisted Matthew Winkler, editor-in-chief of *Bloomberg News*, to write, or help him write, his autobiography. The title was—what else? —*Bloomberg by Bloomberg*.

See if you can tell the difference between the old frat boy, cut-to-the-head-of-the-line Mike and the new statesman Michael R. Bloomberg.

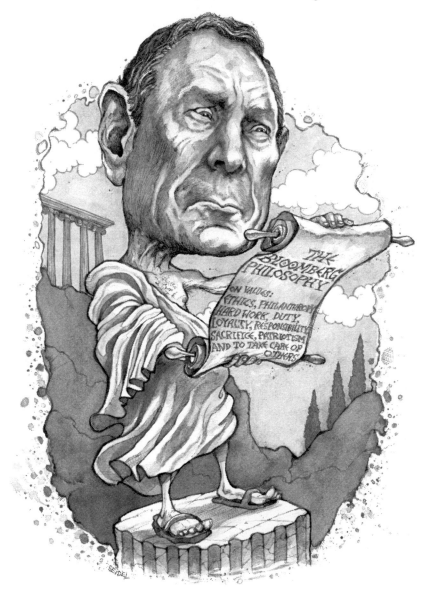

The *Bloomberg by Bloomberg* book jacket describes him as "brash, aggressive, supremely self-confident, hard-hitting with penetrating insight, original thinker ..." and concludes with this uplifting statement: "bon vivant or businessman, Michael Bloomberg has always done it his way."

If Mike, the quintessential "do what ya gotta do" pragmatist, can be said to have a political philosophy, here it is straight from the book:

Those decrying the disparity between the haves and have-nots, and those in government desirous of redistributing wealth [should] take note [that] it is from the rich, in fact, that philanthropic organizations get a disproportionate percentage of their funding. Take notice!

Translation: *It's my money—so piss off.*

CHAPTER TWO

Sniffing Out
City Hall

◄O►

Mike commissioned a political plan for the 2001 mayoral election. The Right People would have to get to know him. He hired publicists, befriended society columnists, and hosted dinner parties for the elite and elaborate costume balls for the semi-elite. The musicians played, the champagne flowed, the performers pranced around on stilts, and the guests stuffed themselves with truffles. The women he dated—he was divorced by now—were thought to be very high class.

Mike didn't ignore the hoi polloi, of course. They voted too. All told, in 2000, he gave more than $100 million to charity, five times more than he had given two years earlier. It was a key part of the plan. Groups such as the United States Hispanic Chamber of Commerce, Asian-American groups, non-profits in Harlem, Bronx, Queens, and Brooklyn all received generous contributions, including the Staten Island Children's Museum and several pro-Israel groups.

Word quickly got around that the little guy was loaded and was giving it away. Mary Holloway of the Association for a Better New York, a business group, called this lavish oiling of the charity social circuits Mike's "favor bank."[17]

He assured skeptics that if he were "lucky enough to be elected," he'd put a "firewall" between the mayor's office and his philanthropy. Mike counts on voters—like customers—to have short memories. So as not to forget, let's jump ahead to examine his firewall right now. Her name is Patti Harris.

Harris used to run Bloomberg LP's Philanthropy, Governmental Affairs, and Public Relations divisions—Money, Lobbying, and Spinning. She was also a key player in Mike's first and subsequent campaigns. Today she is the first deputy mayor and the highest-paid city employee, with a salary of $246,000, not including the $400,000 bonus for consulting on the 2009 election campaign. Moving between Bloomberg LP, City Hall, and his political campaigns is a common practice among Mike's employees. They are paid by the campaigns, the city, the foundations, or whatever mechanisms Mike's lawyers and accountants devise to slip through the legal loopholes.

The "Velvet Hammer," as Patti is known around City Hall, continues doing pretty much what she's always done for Mike: dispensing the cash and minding the politics. "It's ridiculous to think [Mike's] donations have anything to do with politics," she says. Among the directors of his major foundation are Henry M. Paulson, Jr., Jeb Bush, former Miami mayor Manny Diaz, and Newark mayor Cory A. Booker.

Mike's foundation doesn't pay Patti's salary. We do. The five-member, mayoral-appointed Conflicts of Interest Board (COIB) includes real estate lobbyists, recipients of city contracts and grants, and beneficiaries of Mike's philanthropy. It approved the Harris arrangement, apparently adopting Mike's rationale that her work with the foundation "furthers the purpose and interests of the city."

Velvet Hammer or Firewall, Patti phones grantees to ask what they are thinking. What, for example, was a board member of the Metropolitan Museum of Art—Mike is a major donor—thinking about when he bought a couple of $100 tickets to a fund-raiser for someone who was planning to run for mayor in 2005? "The mayor is a loyal friend and he expects loyalty from his friends. It's that simple."[18] Patti isn't Mike's only firewall. When a New York University faculty member criticized Mike's policies, a company official called the dean of the Graduate School of Arts and Sciences to remind her about those journalism fellowships Mike endows. Ed Skyler, who also came over from the company to become a deputy mayor, said, "Like anybody else, the mayor (1) expects to have the support of his friends, but (2) the mayor never holds his personal philanthropy over their heads."[19] The two-part message was carried in the *New York Times*. Which part of the message do you think Mike's grantees didn't understand?

Mike's firewalls will come up again, but let's get back to the events leading up to his first election.

—◄o►—

Mike knew he couldn't win a Democratic primary. But Rudy Giuliani was term limited. Governor George Pataki and a few of his associates owned the Republican ballot line. Mike could buy it. For the primary he would be a Republican; for the general election he would be "Mike, the lifelong Democrat." The newspapers would make it part of his name.

Before he met with Pataki, Mike's advisers likely gave him a quick rundown on the players and what to expect. They would have told him that George Pataki was a creation of US Senator Alfonse D'Amato, or "Fonzie," as he is sometimes affectionately known.

D'Amato, once a town supervisor out in Hempstead, Long Island, emerged from the cesspool of Nassau County Republican politics, where, if you wanted a county job, you kicked back 1 percent of your salary to the Republican political machine. When mobsters were indicted he might make a call to the prosecutor. When they went on trial, he might be up on the witness stand attesting to their good character. Fonzie was considered a very stand-up guy.

A fellow named Joe Margiotta was the county boss. He went to jail. Fonzie went to the US Senate.

Armand D'Amato, the senator's brother, was a lobbyist who worked right out of the senator's offices. When Rudy Giuliani was the US Attorney in Manhattan (D'Amato approved his appointment), he indicted Armand and another high-up D'Amato associate. Word was around that Giuliani might be going after the senator himself. Fonzie went to the mattresses. He backed Ronald Lauder, an heir to the cosmetics fortune, in a Republican mayoral primary campaign against Giuliani. Lauder's negative campaign probably cost Giuliani the 1989 election. David Dinkins, New York's first black mayor, narrowly beat him.

Armand's conviction was later reversed on appeal. Eventually, Fonzie and Rudy made a deal: D'Amato, whose ethical shortcomings had come in for rare criticism by his own senate colleagues, ensured Giuliani a trouble-free path to the Republican nomination in his 1993 rematch against Dinkins. For his part, the prosecutor rented out his reputation to the senator and endorsed him for re-election. The rapprochement was just business. The mayor and the senator despised each other.

It was 1994. D'Amato controlled New York's Republican Party. He tapped George Pataki, then an obscure state senator, to run against Mario Cuomo. With his political base secure, Giuliani sought to get rid of D'Amato and take control of the party. He endorsed Cuomo, telling reporters, "If the D'Amato/Pataki crew ever gets control, ethics will be trashed."

Wrong on the politics, but right about the ethics. Wherever state government intersected with private profits, there you were likely to find D'Amato or one of his associates. Among the most important was Charlie Gargano, D'Amato's chief fundraiser. He became Pataki's chief fundraiser and the head of the Empire State Development Corporation (ESDC).

Real estate developers contributed heavily to Pataki's political campaigns. Through the ESDC and other state agencies, they received tax credits, abatements, and benefits worth billions of dollars. The post–9-11 Liberty Bond program that Congress authorized to help rebuild Lower Manhattan is one of countless examples. The bonds gave developers below-market financing for their projects. Here are four Liberty Bond-financed luxury developments and the political contributions the developers made:

The Solaire was a 293-unit development whose developer gave $10,500 to Pataki and $15,500 to state campaigns. The developer received $235 million worth of Liberty Bonds with an estimated value of $43,065,511.

Liberty Plaza was a 287-unit development whose developers contributed $133,000 to Pataki and an additional $772,000 to statewide campaigns. The developer received $230 million in Liberty Bond financing with an estimated value of $58,642,398.

Tribeca Green was a 274-unit project. The developer gave $54,000 to Pataki and $214,000 to statewide campaigns. The developer received $110 million in Liberty Bonds worth an estimated $20,158,324.

The Historic Front Street Project was a 95-unit development. The developer contributed $70,000 to Pataki and $456,000 to state campaigns. The developer received $46.3 million in Liberty Bonds worth an estimated $8,484,000.[20]

It wasn't only the developers: an investment in George Pataki's career yielded fabulous returns for many people who did business with the state. Libby Pataki, the governor's wife, who hadn't worked in decades, took in hundreds of thousands of dollars annually as a consultant.

To supplement his government salary, state senator Pataki had maintained a small law office in Peekskill, New York. After 12 years as governor, he was a multimillionaire.

◄O►

That's the short version of what Mike's advisers might have told him. Ethics wasn't the issue that concerned Mike. What was legal and what wasn't—yes, of course. But Mike is a numbers guy. He just wanted to know how much. And if the corruption was as pervasive as Giuliani had predicted it would be, how much could it cost? Whatever the price, it wouldn't even be a rounding number in Mike's personal balance sheet.

A Republican Makeover

Mike and George met. A deal was cut. They didn't hold a press conference.

We do know that before the election, Mike gave various Republican entities in the state a down payment of at least $300,000 and quickly became the party's #1 financier. He's donated many millions to Republican state, federal, and local politicians since becoming mayor. Even Tom DeLay got some. But cash was only the ante. He'd still need voters. The first thing he'd have to do was to take care of his Jewish problem.

It seems that in 1995, before he'd been thinking about electoral politics, Mike told an interviewer for the *Jewish Report*, an Israeli magazine, that he had "no particular desire to visit Israel, that you don't spend time davening [praying], and that if I don't call God, he won't call me."[21]

It was just Mike being Mike. Surely people would understand it was only a joke. But the killer was this line: "I won't give too much money to the UJA because of the hold the religious have on Israel. I have one wish: Shoot all the clerics."

Orthodox Jews are like the National Rifle Association: They vote as a bloc. What the Grand Rabbi says goes. He wasn't known for his sense of humor when it came to Israel. What to do?

Mike took his very first trip to the Holy Land in January 2001. *Bloomberg Floating on the Dead Sea. Bloomberg Meeting the Israeli Prime Minister. Bloomberg Shaking Hands with the Mayor of Jerusalem.*[22] Mike came back from his pilgrimage refreshed and ready to meet his co-religionists. He had become a Zionist.[23]

"*I have always believed that the fate of Israel and the future of New York are deeply connected.... ... A strong Israel means a strong America and a strong New York.*"

The room was a bit stuffy and crowded, but Mike's performance was outstanding. He'd have no problem with the Orthodox Jews, but of course he still had plenty of work to do. To begin with, he'd need a second line on the ballot.

Mike's Kinky Political Bedfellows

The Independence Party line was available. It came with some baggage. Created to get Ross Perot on the New York state ballot for the 1992 presidential election, the New York City wing of the party was controlled by Fred Newman, the founder of a "social therapy" movement that he called "friendosexuality." He was a randy fellow who slept with his patients and got them to turn over their assets. He also founded the International Workers Party.[24] Mike might have been okay with the sex and money, but he didn't go in for that Marxist crap.

Newman stayed in the background. The party's public face belonged to Lenora Fulani, his disciple. A not unattractive black woman who called herself a "developmental psychologist," Fulani said Jews were "the bloodsuckers of the world" and "mass murderers of people of color." (Newman and his organization had briefly joined the anti-Semitic Lyndon LaRouche cult in 1974. In 1992 his cultural front group put on his play titled *Dead as a Jew*.) Fulani was a favorite of Louis Farrakhan. Mike was undeterred.

He was getting the hang of this democracy thing. Fulani wouldn't retract anything she had said about Jews, but she quieted down in public. Newman, Mike thought, was a little kinky, but a nice enough old geezer.

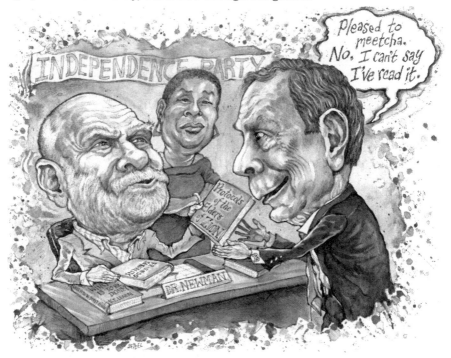

Mike became the Independence Party's chief financier, its rabbi so to speak. When challenged about his association with such unsavory characters, he said Fulani's comments about Jews were despicable, but she was only one member of the party. Robert Goodkind, president of the American Jewish Committee, wrote the *New York Times* that "if David Duke were a leading figure in a Louisiana third party, no one in New York would accept such an excuse from politicians eager to take that ballot line." The *Times* didn't publish the letter.

◄o►

Staten Island, the heartland of the Republican and Conservative parties, was next on Mike's to-do list. The former and soon-to-be police commissioner Ray Kelly had observed that no important project gets done on Staten Island without the mob's involvement. The Genoveses and the Gambinos, the Colombos and the Bonannos, Big Paulie Castellano—all the families were out there. George Pataki raised a lot of money in Staten Island. Reporters were always pestering him about it. Pataki said his contributors were just "political friends."

None of that weasel stuff for Mike: "Jimmy Molinaro [the Conservative Party boss who became borough president in 2002] is the most honest and trustworthy person I have ever met."[25]

Mike felt just as warmly toward Guy Molinari, the Republican Staten Island borough president, Molinaro's predecessor. Molinari and Molinaro were good friends. Molinari's law partner was also Molinaro's executive assistant.

Molinari spearheaded a large warehouse development as part of a port renewal project. He put at least a million dollars of borough government funds into it.

Salvatore Calcagno, Molinaro's campaign finance chairman, got a big trucking contract from Carmine Ragucci, who ran the port.

Molinaro's son, Steven, was Calcagno's business partner, and Molinaro himself was partners with Calcagno in a Florida real estate deal. Federal prosecutors said Calcagno, who was convicted of tax fraud, laundered millions of dollars by making out phony checks to subcontractors.[26]

At a federal racketeering trial, a government witness testified that he watched Ragucci each month stuff $9,200 into brown envelopes and give the envelopes to Anthony "Sonny" Ciccone, a Gambino captain. According to federal prosecutors, Ragucci is a Gambino associate. When Molinaro stepped down as Conservative Party chairman to run for borough president, he named Ragucci as his successor.[27]

Jimmy Molinaro is the most honest and trustworthy guy Mike has ever met.

—◄○►—

Marxism, Black Nationalism, anti-Semitism, Zionism, the Mob—Mike was determined to be mayor and nothing was going to stop him.

He was slogging through a Spanish-language course when he learned that Herman Badillo, the country's first Puerto Rican congressman, was going to run against him in the Republican primary.

Badillo had tried five times to win the mayoralty as a Democrat. He had finally given up and ran for city comptroller as a Republican in 1993. He lost and became a real estate lobbyist. Now it was 2001—time to saddle up.[28]

Veteran New York political reporter Gabe Pressman moderated their televised debate. He questioned Mike about the sexual-harassment stories and the "Wit and Wisdom" booklet. Mike was ready:

(1) If anybody was offended, I apologize; (2) I had nothing to do with the book that was given to me; (3) I don't remember. It happened ten years ago; (4) it comes up three days before a primary—come on, that's just

normal politics, so I'm told. I'm not a politician. And finally (5) I didn't say those things. I didn't write the book.

Whew.

Bloomberg: "Nobody alleges that I said this. It was in a book written by somebody else. Let's go on to the issues. Come on …"

Badillo: "The *Daily News* reports today that Mr. Bloomberg's lawyers, Willkie Farr & Gallagher, have threatened her [Elizabeth DeMarse, the employee who presented the book] and told her not to open her mouth … I call upon Mr. Bloomberg to call his lawyers off. Let the woman who wrote the book tell the public who you really are."

Bloomberg: "We're not going to do it … don't even waste your time asking."[29]

In the only other debate, hosted by NPR's Brian Lehrer, Mike explained how he had ended up on the Republican line. "Well, I was a Democrat. The Republican Party and the Independence Party both came to me."

How could he say no?

Lehrer: "Mr. Bloomberg, do you have a question for Mr. Badillo?"

Mike was ready for that one. His handlers had put the inner Mike on a tight leash during the campaign. Sinking his teeth into Badillo, who couldn't win a Republican primary anyway, wouldn't sit well with Hispanic voters.

Bloomberg: "Sure. Will you join my administration if I'm fortunate enough to become mayor of the city? I'd love to have the benefit of your wisdom, and I think you could be a big plus to my administration. And I'd like to know, would you do it?"

You want humble, Herman? I can do humble, you son of a bitch.

While Mike was busy buying the ballot lines, the consultants and image makers, the television time, and so on, the world was focused on the aftermath of 9-11. Like most New Yorkers, I had never heard of Michael Bloomberg. My neighbors and I had been under siege for two years before the twin towers went down. Our struggle with the owner of our complex and the politicians and housing officials who supported him is a good lens through which to view the debased political and media culture that made Mike possible.

Independence Plaza

For the past 25 years or so, my wife and I have lived in a 3,500-person affordable housing development in Lower Manhattan known as Independence Plaza. The three 39-story towers and the 69 low-rise attached brick buildings that run between them overlook the Hudson River a few blocks north of Ground Zero. It was built under a New York program popularly known as Mitchell-Lama.

Despite decades of corruption and profiteering, Mitchell-Lama was one of the nation's most successful housing programs. It delivered approximately 141,000 units of affordable housing in New York City and brought back scores of declining neighborhoods.

The tenants in our development were black, white, Hispanic, Asian—hyphenated Americans of virtually every demographic. Integrated housing along race and class lines is rare in New York, or anywhere, for that matter. For Mitchell-Lama developments it was common.

Most tenants were of moderate income and some 20 percent were poor. Mitchell-Lama had income-eligibility limits for people trying to get an apartment. The waiting list numbered in the thousands. Families whose household incomes rose above the entry-level limits after they moved in weren't kicked out; instead, they paid a surcharge of up to double the regulated rent, still less than market rate. That policy was a key factor in maintaining the integrated nature of our complex. If you're not rich and you have an affordable apartment in New York City, you don't move. (Most people who moved to the city during the Giuliani-Bloomberg era don't realize how much easier it was to find an affordable place to live before then.) We were a friendly and stable community.

The neighborhood had been New York's principal food depot dating back to colonial days. As the food merchants moved out, artists began moving into the empty commercial lofts. Where artists go, real estate operators are never far behind. When they turn your neighborhood into an acronym—Soho, Noho, Dumbo, Nolita, Spaha—watch out: The neighborhood will change and you'd better start looking for another place to live.

Sometime during the Giuliani years in the 1990s, the locally owned stores and restaurants began giving way to multimillion-dollar lofts, designer restaurants, and high-end antique shops. We became TriBeCa—the Triangle Below Canal Street— one of the highest-priced real estate markets in the country. At night, we began seeing the stretch limousines double parked in front of Robert De Niro's various enterprises: Nobu, Tribeca Grill, and most recently the Greenwich Hotel, with suites at $5,500 a night. It was happening all around us. We were rent regulated and had nothing to worry about, or so we thought.

◄o►

Some of the neighborhood's newcomers referred to Independence Plaza as "the projects." Suddenly, it began to feel that way. Elevators broke down. Old hallway carpeting was rarely vacuumed, let alone replaced. The plumbing went haywire, and toilets overflowed, flooding the apartments below. At night neighborhood thugs would stage pit bull fights in the concrete courtyards behind the low-rise apartments.

Harold Cohn, the owner-builder, fired all the union doormen and replaced them with hourly workers. His new security chief was an ex-cop who had been thrown off the force for, among other things, beating up and hospitalizing a 64-year-old woman. It's not easy to get thrown off the NYPD for brutality. An air of intimidation hung over Independence Plaza. It didn't feel like home any more. We didn't yet know that was what Harold Cohn and his partners had in mind.

◄o►

A small group of us got together and decided to run for the tenant board, which wasn't dealing with the deteriorating conditions. I was retired by then and had never gone to a tenant meeting. But nobody wanted to be board president. John Scott, a long-time community activist, said, "Neil, if you run for president, I'll be vice-president." I agreed, reluctantly. In the summer of 2000, as Giuliani's second term was winding down, the new board was elected.

Tenants too frightened to sign their names began sending me letters about the aggressive and threatening new doormen, one of whom rang my bell and Scott's after midnight, ostensibly to deliver a memorandum from management. We complained to the city's housing regulators about the intimidation, harassment, and deteriorating conditions, and we asked them to replace the $750,000-a-year management firm owned by Harold Cohn's nephew. Giuliani's housing regulators stonewalled us.

At first, we didn't know that Harold Cohn could exit the Mitchell-Lama affordable housing program and with some capital improvements and cosmetic changes, could raise the rent roll from about $12 million to $36 million, maybe more. Lower-income tenants would qualify for federal housing vouchers. They would pay a third of their incomes toward the new, Tribeca-based rents, and the federal government would pay two-thirds. In other words, these tenants, perhaps as many as half of them, would be the medium through which Cohn would collect federally guaranteed, market-based rents—for as long as Congress appropriated the housing voucher money. The rest of the tenants could either pay the new rents or move.

Or Cohn could sell Independence Plaza and someone else could do the wet work of evicting tenants, litigating, politicking, and all the rest of it. This was all news to us—until we began reading newspaper accounts of developments like ours being taken out of the program and rents being doubled and more.

The right to exit the program was based on an obscure amendment to the original Mitchell-Lama law passed in Albany more than thirty years earlier. The Mitchell-Lama landlords and the housing regulators knew about it, but they never told the people who lived in the developments. It wasn't in our leases, not even in the fine print.

In 2000, a rent-regulated Independence Plaza was valued at about $150 million. A deregulated Independence Plaza might be worth $400 million or more in the hot Tribeca market, a huge payday even by New York real estate standards where multimillion-dollar profits are common.

When we understood that what was at stake wasn't maintenance and repairs, as important as those were, but losing our homes, things took on an even greater sense of urgency; we spent the next year organizing and raising money.

The toxic landlord–tenant relationship in New York is a thing of legend. Hiring thugs to intimidate tenants, throwing acid in their faces, introducing rats into rent-regulated buildings, all of these things are well-documented. That's not to suggest that all or even most landlords will go to such extremes, but there we were with thugs for security guards and a vast amount of money at stake. I told the tenants not to focus on Cohn. We knew what he wanted to do—maximize his profits—and there was nothing we could do about that. The only thing that mattered was whether politicians who could help us would do so. Many tenants refused to believe that the "powers that be" would allow thousands of people to be put under such pressure by one person. It was hard to explain the facts of political life to people who had never paid much attention to politics.

Then the World Trade Center went down. We watched in shock as the second plane hit, saw the people running beneath our windows, and watched a tower collapse a few blocks away. Our neighborhood was a disaster. It looked as though it might not come back for years. The people who lived in our southernmost tower were forced to evacuate for months. Our future in New York, let alone at Independence Plaza, seemed bleak.

CHAPTER THREE

Racing to
the Bottom

◄O►

The mayoral primaries were already underway when the planes hit that morning. They were rescheduled for September 25. There was likely to be a Democratic runoff for the nomination. The eventual winner would have to raise considerably more money and turn out his core supporters three times. And now Mike had a convincing rationale: *In this time of crisis, New York needs a manager, not a politician.* That message meshed nicely with "I want to give something back. I've been lucky." Mike was a humble billionaire. But he had a way to go to get to be mayor on the Republican line in a 5-1 Democratic town. And it wasn't only the Democratic opposition who stood in his way.

In the weeks and months that followed, Rudy Giuliani transcended politics. Oprah hailed him as "America's Mayor." Before 9-11, his approval ratings had dropped from the high 70s to the mid-30s. What with his notorious nastiness, the extramarital relationships, the police killings of innocent black people, and all the rest of it, not even prostate cancer had made him a sympathetic figure. And if large segments of the public didn't like him, insiders detested him. Ed Koch had even taken a break from turning out paperback accounts of his own wonderfulness to write a book titled, *Giuliani: Nasty Man.*

Many New Yorkers still remembered Rudy's 1992 cheerleading speech to thousands of off-duty, beer-drinking, menacing cops who blocked the entrance to City Hall, tied up traffic on the Brooklyn Bridge, rocked cars, shouted "nigger," and threatened people. The cops wanted a new collective-bargaining agreement, and they didn't much care for David Dinkins. They waived signs like "Dump the Washroom Attendant" and "Dinkins Sucks" with pictures of a thick-lipped, Afro-wearing mayor. The jubilant Rudy, who was there (and now says he was trying to calm the situation), called Dinkins' civilian review board proposal "bullshit." The cops cheered "Rudy! Rudy! Rudy!"

In those years, Al Sharpton was out and about with his patented chant, "No Justice, No Peace." But the squeegee men were off the streets, and even people who had had enough of Rudy gave him credit for that. Mike needed his endorsement.

But America's Mayor was in no hurry to endorse anyone. In fact, he was in no hurry to leave. He too had a rationale: *New York needs me.* Days after the terrorist attack, he launched his campaign to overturn term limits. Wherever he went, "spontaneous" crowds followed him chanting "four more years" into the TV cameras.

It was too late for city council legislation to overturn term limits. But the state legislature and the governor could do it. If Albany didn't give him a three-month extension, Rudy said, he'd run for a full term on the Conservative Party line. *Whatever Rudy wants is okay with me,* was George Pataki's public stance; ditto for Mike and for Mark Green, the Public Advocate who emerged from the primary as one of the two remaining Democratic candidates. Nobody wanted to alienate

Rudy. They were shouldering each other out of the way for a spot alongside him on speaking platforms near Ground Zero.

Only Bronx Borough President Fernando Ferrer, the other Democrat in the race, wouldn't go along. In early October, Assembly Speaker Sheldon Silver said the Albany Democrats wouldn't consider extending Rudy's term. Rudy was bluffing about the Conservative Party line. He'd come around as soon as Mike won the Republican primary, which he did easily. It was Herman Badillo's last hurrah.

Mark Green narrowly defeated Ferrer in the nasty Democratic runoff. I met with Green's top staff people to discuss the Independence Plaza situation. Green's brother, a large real estate operator, was heading his fundraising operation. As with all New York politicians, Green was raising money from the real estate lobby. If elected, he would do nothing for us.

I urged tenants to support Bloomberg. I didn't know anything about him, but it was enough to know that he didn't need the real estate money.

Mike was ready to roll. *Monday Night Football, Frasier, Who Wants to Be a Millionaire, Family Law, Wheel of Fortune, Dateline NBC*—he even bought 60-second spots for the ninth inning of the World Series. Was anybody else even running?

Green came out of the primary with a 40-point lead in the polls. It evaporated overnight. "I'm not a professional politician," Mike told reporters. "I intend to finance my own campaign. I won't ask special interests for a dime." He wasn't buying an election; he was simply financing his own campaign. Green was short on cash and likeability—even the *New York Times*, which endorsed him, said he "has not been the most lovable candidate in New York City history."

—◁○▻—

Well-known political consultants swarmed around Mike like flies around an open garbage can. Doug Schoen, Bill Clinton's pollster, and David Garth, who had been media strategist for John Lindsay, Koch, and Giuliani, were perhaps the best known consultants. But there were dozens of others. Mike even brought in the baby-faced Frank Luntz, who'd built a career coaching Washington's Republican knuckle-draggers how to defeat inheritance taxes (call them "death taxes" and hold press conferences in funeral parlors), privatize social security (don't say "privatize," say "personalize"), deal with concerns over global warming by using the less-threatening "climate change" and claim that scientists still question the science. Healthcare reform? Simple: Don't let Washington put a bureaucrat between you and your doctor.

Luntz was Mike's kind of guy.

Rudy's operatic try for a third term having failed, he finally met with Mike and David Garth in a private room at a Manhattan steakhouse. By the time they tucked into their steaks, they had a deal. Garth transformed the tepid statement into a ring-ing endorsement: "New York Loves Rudy and Rudy Loves Mike." As with Giuliani's earlier D'Amato endorsement, this one was just business.

New Yorkers wanted to come together after 9-11, but the racial and ethnic undercurrents of city politics are never far from the surface and thus never far from the thinking of political consultants and their clients. If stirring the racial pot gives a political advantage, the pot will be stirred. A little bit of history helps put what follows in its proper context.

Years before the September 1992 off-duty police riot described earlier, there had been a watershed moment in the city's racial politics. It was 1968, during John Lindsay's first term as mayor. Controversial state legislation had taken some pow-ers from the central board of education and given them to local school boards. The black-controlled school board in the Ocean Hill–Brownsville section of Brooklyn sought to transfer ten Jewish teachers out of the district. Amid charges and counter-charges of racism, anti-Semitism, and union busting, Albert Shanker, the head of the teachers' union, a majority of whose members were Jewish, called a citywide strike, shutting down the public schools for more than a month. (In Woody Allen's movie *Sleeper*, a Rip Van Winkle character wakes up 200 years into the future to find a barren landscape. He asks a stranger what happened and is told that Western civilization ended when a man named Albert Shanker got his hands on the bomb. Woody Allen graduated from Midwood High School in Brooklyn in 1953, a year ahead of me.)

The Ocean Hill–Brownsville episode ripped apart the already frayed relation-ships between New York's blacks and Jews and between whites and blacks more generally. Though they were considered more liberal than other ethnic groups, Jews, especially those who lived outside of Manhattan, watched the Ocean Hill–Brownsville fight, read about a crude mimeographed anti-Semitic screed (dupli-cated and distributed in Albany by the teachers' union), and became more closely aligned with conservative, working- and middle-class Catholics, the majority of whom also sided with the union. A white backlash that had begun with opposition to the creation of a civilian review board to handle police-brutality complaints—a proposal that Dinkins would later revive—became much more pronounced after Ocean Hill–Brownsville.

Whether it is smoldering beneath the surface or is a raging fire, as it was under Lindsay, Dinkins, Koch, and Giuliani (with Rupert Murdoch's *New York Post* pour-ing on the gasoline), race is always a dominant factor in New York politics. The 2001 mayoral campaign was no exception. Some of Green's supporters distributed a flyer that depicted Freddy Ferrer kissing the behind of a grotesque Al Sharpton.[30] Prominent Jewish figures published a letter in the *Jewish Press* that blamed Ferrer for "dividing the city racially." They accused Sharpton of inciting a mob against Hasidic Jews during the infamous 1991 Crown Heights episode.

Wilbert Tatum, owner of the *Amsterdam News*, the city's largest black-owned paper, endorsed Bloomberg and railed at "the gang of Jews from Brooklyn." Mike had learned how to handle that problem. "I accept the endorsement, but I would have used different words." In their final debate, Mike went for the jugular.

Bloomberg: "Mark, isn't it time that you apologize for the smearing of Freddy Ferrer, saying that he was borderline irresponsible? Isn't it time to say 'enough,' that you should not have had or somebody should not have, in your interest, put out these disgraceful fliers and made those disgraceful calls? And will you promise right now to stop this politics of personal destruction that you seem to do every time you get close in an election?"

Green: "This is a man who said two weeks ago he wouldn't raise these issues because it's racially divisive. So what's despicable is the hypocrisy you just heard."

Mike was just warming up.

Television ads featured blacks and Hispanics criticizing Green for "dividing the people with his negative campaigning." Mark Green was being transformed into Lester Maddox.

New York Times columnist Bob Herbert called Mike out:

Even as the Democrats were trying to pull themselves out of the slough of racial politics, Mr. Bloomberg was finding new and creative ways to crawl in ... What the ad shows is that Mr. Bloomberg is as opportunistic and hypocritical as any professional pol ... And after running this blatantly racially exploitive ad, he stood before reporters over the weekend and solemnly proclaimed, "Nobody should be discussing race whatsoever."[31]

Al Sharpton, the grandmaster of racial politics, didn't appreciate Mike messing with his franchise. "Bloomberg is playing hardball in my ballpark," he said, pointing out Mike's memberships in several no-blacks-need-apply social clubs. Pointedly, Sharpton didn't attack Mike's membership in the most notorious whites-only club of all, the New York State Republican Party, where black people rarely if ever rise above the level of secretary, but where the occasional clergyman–politician who is black can be found feeding at the Republican patronage trough. Apparently Reverend Al thought he could do business with Mike. He announced that he was leaving for Israel. "I am going to the Wailing Wall to promise God that I will not support Mark Green for mayor." And he went.

Mike's Staten Island campaign office distributed leaflets that displayed pictures of Green and David Dinkins. The leaflets warned that Green's election would mean a return to the Dinkins era. He would do something similar in the 2009 campaign. He assured reporters that he thought the leaflets were "outrageous."

Poor Freddy Ferrer: Mike and Al Sharpton were way out of his league. Ferrer held a news conference with Green, calling Mike's campaign cynical and exploitive. Mike flooded Hispanic neighborhoods with glossy campaign literature that featured Ferrer's picture. Ferrer and his inner circle were outraged, but who cared? Mike's spokesman, Bill Cunningham, demanded that Green take a lie-detector test about his campaign literature!

Mike ran full-page ads in the *Amsterdam News*, *El Diario/La Prensa*, the *Daily Gleaner*, and other ethnic newspapers. His four-page color insert in the Yiddish newspaper *Der Tzitung* promised 100,000 affordable apartments and included a map that featured neighborhoods with heavy Jewish populations. It was the city's traditional political alchemy—transforming ad revenues in ethnic newspapers into editorial endorsements.

Large numbers of glossy booklets arrived in selected mailboxes around the city. They described how Mike had become the first Jew admitted to his college fraternity, and "one of the Jewish community's most dedicated volunteers and most generous donors." How many booklets were mailed or who received them was a secret. Bill Cunningham said, "I would imagine this hit a pretty broad spectrum of people who live throughout the city."[32]

But even with Sharpton at the Wailing Wall beseeching the Hebrew God, Mike desperately needed moderate-liberal white voters.

Bill Keller, then the *New York Times* op-ed editor, heard the call.

His 1,432-word essay was a veritable ode to Mike. It was "not an endorsement of the candidacy of Michael Bloomberg," Keller assured his readers. "For endorsements, you have to go next door to the editorial page, where, if you are a candidate encumbered by great wealth, you may be subjected to the Biblical eye-of-the-needle test. This is an endorsement of the idea of Michael Bloomberg, meaning the idea that it would not kill us to have a few self-made billionaires in our political life."

Keller fulminated against cynical journalists and asked, "Why shouldn't the rich work for us? … When someone comes along who talks about 'giving back,' and seems to believe it, why is that not cause for celebration?"[33]

Bill Keller had gone for the razzle![34] The high-fives at campaign headquarters could be heard all around New York.

CHAPTER FOUR

Top Dog

—◦—

On November 6, 2001, Mike scratched out a 744,000 to 709,000 win. At last! Manhattan's well-off election districts—*New York Times* readers—had been as important to the victory as the Independence Party line. Keller's op-ed piece has been long forgotten, but reporters who worked at the paper didn't have to be reminded. Keller, the son of a former chairman of Chevron Oil Company, would be named executive editor of the *Times* in July 2003. Over the years, the *Times* has been instrumental in establishing Keller's Idea of Mike—the nonpartisan public servant just giving something back.

I was pleased that Giuliani and Green were gone—and hopeful. Along with most New Yorkers, I didn't know who Mike was or what policies he'd pursue. He wasn't about to tell us.

◄○►

With the ruins of the Twin Towers still smoldering, *Mayor Helicopters to the Hamptons* wasn't the ink his handlers wanted. He had spent tens of millions of dollars on the Bloomberg brand, but for voters he was "Mike," the regular guy who prefers hamburgers to filet mignon.

He could change the name by which the public would know him but not his nature. Eventually, reporters—and through them the public—would sense the inauthenticity of Humble Mike. They'd believe "tough," "resolute," that kind of thing; *New York is a tough city. We need a tough mayor. Mike may be a prick, but he's our prick.* Smart politics.

He wouldn't change his lifestyle either. Mike had worked hard for his money. He wanted to enjoy it. His handlers would have to tone it down, though, and keep the public from viewing him as the guy who flew by private jet to Bermuda and helicoptered to the Hamptons.

Soon, New Yorkers began seeing pictures of Mike riding the subway, a New York Times folded lengthways like a real New Yorker. *Newsday* even called him "Regular Joe Commuter."

And so while George W. cut brush in Crawford, Mike became a New York straphanger. *Imagine, the mayor rides the subway to work just like us!* Interviewed by Jon Stewart years later, he told a story about a stranger who came up to his table to talk about an issue while "I was having dinner with my girlfriend, you know, a hamburger, a pickle, and a chip." Stewart hadn't asked him what he was eating. Mike had completely internalized the script. It's a small detail, that hamburger, pickle, and chip, but it speaks to the impressive energy and focus of the determined little guy. He was selling "Mike" and with Bill Keller and the *New York Times* pushing the image, a lot of people were buying—and still are.

Selling Racial Harmony

Mike had managed to avoid much criticism for playing the race card during the campaign. Now that he was mayor, the post–9-11 zeitgeist called for a uniter, not a divider. The morning after the election, accompanied by reporters and photographers, Mike went to the Bronx to have breakfast with Freddie Ferrer.

In the weeks and months following the election, there was scarcely a black or Hispanic clergyman, politician, or labor leader of any importance who didn't get a visit or a phone call. After eight years of the pugnacious and racially divisive Giuliani, New Yorkers applauded the new civil tone coming out of City Hall.

Al Sharpton, back from the Wailing Wall, was hosting a Martin Luther King Day party at his National Action Network headquarters. Mike did a drop-in. Sharpton, who had been barred from Rudy's City Hall, would soon become Mike's "favorite civil rights leader."

Eight years later, Mike was still being praised for "reaching out." Mark Naison, a professor of African American studies at Fordham University, for example, had this to say in October 2009:

> *I think Bloomberg has been very effective at reaching out to black leaders.*
> *... He's also built up a relationship with people like Al Sharpton and others around school issues.*[35]

Before explaining how Mike neutered Sharpton and other black leaders, let me give the Reverend his due: For decades, the Baptist minister had led protest marches through the city's white neighborhoods. A few episodes speak to his role in the pre-Bloomberg era.

On December 20, 1986, three young black men stalled their car near Howard Beach, Queens. A group of white thugs armed with baseball bats and tire irons beat them mercilessly. One victim staggered out onto a six-lane expressway and was killed by an oncoming car. Sharpton led the protest marches. Howard Beach residents chanted "Niggers … niggers … niggers …"

In August 1989, a group of white thugs set upon four black teenagers in Bensonhurst, Brooklyn, and murdered 16-year-old Yusuf Hawkins, who had come to the neighborhood to buy a used car. Sharpton led a march through Bensonhurst. Residents shouted, "Niggers go home" and held up watermelons. One of them stabbed Sharpton in the chest, nearly killing him.

In 1991, in Crown Heights, Brooklyn, the 7-year-old son of Guyanese immigrants was killed when a car in a Hasidic Jewish rabbi's motorcade ran up onto the sidewalk. Jews and blacks hurled rocks and bottles at each other for four days. A visiting Jewish student from Australia was stabbed to death amidst cries of "Kill the Jew." Sharpton led marchers to the headquarters of the Lubavitcher Hasidic sect, chanting "No justice, no peace!" "If the Jews want to get it on," he shouted, "tell them to pin their yarmulkes back and come over to my house."

In 1995, Sharpton led a demonstration against the eviction of a black-owned record store in Harlem. "We will not stand by and allow them to move this brother so that some white interloper can expand his business," he shouted. One of the protesters set the store on fire and shot and killed himself, along with several customers.

The most notorious police killing during the Giuliani years came in 1999 when four plainclothes cops fired 41 full-metal-jacket bullets at a wholly innocent Amadou Diallo. They said they thought the wallet he was reaching for was a gun. Sharpton led the protests and was arrested with other prominent New Yorkers, David Dinkins among them.

Reverend Al is a decidedly mixed bag. There's the brilliant orator-organizer who put his body on the line when black people were being murdered and abused, and there's the Tawana Brawley, race-baiting hustler who has been investigated, indicted, acquitted, and fined many times, and whose personal financial records have gone up in flames more than once.

He's earned the praise and the scorn. Mike only has praise.

Al Sharpton has been an awful lot more of a calming influence on the city and helper to the city than most people give him credit for. I don't agree with him on everything, but on balance I've become, over the years, a Sharpton fan.[36]

Neutering Al Sharpton

We don't know everything, or even very much, about what goes on between Mike and Al, but from what we do know about each man, we can be sure that money is the tie that binds them. The following episode is a window onto the relationship. In June 2008, Sharpton and Joel Klein, Mike's schools chancellor, announced the formation of the Education Equality Project (EEP), a campaign to close the educational achievement gap between white and black children. Former *Daily News* education reporter Joe Williams was EEP's president.

A hedge fund headed by former chancellor Harold Levy put $500,000 into the tax-exempt entity, which then moved the money to Sharpton's National Action Network. Levy's hedge fund invests in gambling businesses. He was lobbying Mike for a role in New York's Off-Track Betting Corporation. He was also helping to finance a billion-dollar bid for the Aqueduct Racetrack redevelopment project in Queens, a stink bomb that involved the Rev. Floyd Flake.

Levy bristled at the suggestion that the $500,000 was a "way of currying favor with anyone." He told the *Daily News*, "The collaboration between Rev. Sharpton and Chancellor Klein is a novel alliance that we thought might help raise the visibility of [high-poverty schools]."

Sharpton wasn't "necessarily" for more mayoral control of the public schools, but, "The nation's future is at stake." He drew down a second $500,000 from two $250,000 contributions EEP received from "Anonymous." Mike was one of those two donors, almost certainly both. Joe Williams referred all money questions to Klein and Sharpton.

Following the $1 million grant, Sharpton made a down payment to the IRS. The US Attorney then dropped his investigation of the federal matching funds that Sharpton had received in connection with his Democratic presidential primary race, a race managed and financed by notorious Republican dirty trickster Roger Stone. Reverend Sharpton is a first-class passenger on Mike's Gravy Train.

—◄○►—

Reverend Calvin Butts, minister of Harlem's legendary Abyssinian Baptist Church, is also a "show me the money" guy. Before Mike came along, he had been drinking out of the Albany fire hose for years. As with Sharpton, Rudy had shut him out of City Hall. Butts had tried to make amends for his criticism of Giuliani's policies regarding black people but Rudy had positioned himself as the Mayor Who Would Restore Law and Order—read crack down on black crime—and he was implacable. Butts also was barred from City Hall. George Pataki appointed him to the state's Economic Development Corporation. With Pataki's support, the Abyssinian Development Corporation, the church's real estate arm, became one of Harlem's most important developers.

Pataki also installed Butts as the president of the State University of New York campus at Old Westbury, giving him a six-figure salary on top of his Abyssinian earnings. Reverend Butts endorsed Pataki's re-election and hosted prayer breakfasts for him. Mike's public position on race gave Butts and other black clergymen-politicians room to support him and maintain their credibility and they did. Mike skipped the prayer breakfasts and poured millions of public and private dollars into the church and its real estate arm. Butts became a fervent Mike supporter. He assured his followers: "The money has nothing to do with my political support. Nobody buys my loyalty."

—◄○►—

Reverend Floyd Flake, a former congressman, headed the 25,000-member Allen African Methodist Episcopal Church in Queens. He too ran a large real estate operation. Over the years, Flake has been embroiled in various money scandals. An ally of Al D'Amato's, and a Pataki and Giuliani supporter, Reverend Flake soon became one of Mike's favorite politician-clergymen.[37] Mike put him on the city's Economic Development Board and in his second campaign went over to the church to receive praises from the pulpit.[38]

Rev. Clinton M. Miller, pastor of Brown Memorial Baptist Church in Brooklyn, summed it up nicely: "Who do I trust more, in terms of how I am going to get my projects done? The choice is between a municipality and God."[39]

Mike needed only a small portion of his wealth to gain office. Once in, he leveraged his money with ours to stay there.

The Independence Party had delivered 59,000 votes in an election decided by 35,000. He'd need the line again. Mike delivered some $8.7 million in tax-exempt financing from the New York City Industrial Development Agency and another $4 million for the All-Stars project, a performing arts center for kids. Millions more of Mike's personal money went into the party's housekeeping account.[40]

Every elected politician rewards friends and punishes enemies. It's the scale of payoffs and the careless cruelty toward those who don't count that make Mike special.

He had occupied City Hall for a year. He hadn't replaced Giuliani's housing regulators and they continued to stonewall us. Mike had a plan for the city, and tenants who lived in rent-regulated housing weren't part of it.

CHAPTER FIVE

Mike's Luxury City:
Hamptons on the Hudson

—◄o►—

Most mayors and governors can do little more than react to events they don't control. Mike's own fortune, his network of the richest and most powerful New Yorkers, and the powers vested in the city's strong mayor system enabled him to pursue a much larger agenda than any mayor before him.

Here is Harvard's Susan Fainstein:

Michael R. Bloomberg and his deputy mayor for economic development, Daniel L. Doctoroff, have ambitions for remaking much of the city on a scale comparable to the remaking overseen by Robert Moses in the 1940s and 1950s. ... "We," Doctoroff said, "have big, long-term visions. That's why we sometimes speak in billions, not millions ... and why our horizon stretches for decades, not months." [41]

Mike thought of himself then, maybe still does, as a modern-day Robert Moses, who also dominated the politicians of his day. Moses conceived, planned, constructed, and financed the parks, bridges, tunnels, expressways, sports stadiums, and urban renewal projects that shape New York to this day. As with Mike, Moses had discretion over vast sums of money. The money belonged to the public authorities he controlled, but that was a technicality. Answerable only to the bondholders who cared only about the tax-free interest payments on their bonds, Moses brooked no criticism from mayors, governors, or even presidents.

As he went about destroying countless working-class neighborhoods and uprooting the lives of hundreds of thousands of people, he enjoyed the support of the city's newspapers.

Eventually, Moses went too far. His efforts to ram a four-lane highway through the middle of Washington Square Park; a Lower Manhattan Expressway through SoHo, Little Italy, Chinatown, and the Lower East Side; and, probably most important, his midnight bulldozing of a Central Park play area used by the kids of upper-middle-class and wealthy residents for an 80-car parking lot was the beginning of the end. His press support finally eroded and the public began to see the arrogant bully beneath the doer of big deeds. Still, it took the only other person who combined vast wealth with political and governmental power to take him down: Nelson Rockefeller, our last mega-billionaire politician. "Rocky" was a knish-eating campaigner who also ran up huge debts, destroyed working class neighborhoods, and built sterile monuments to his memory. He will reappear later in this book.[42]

Late in Mike's third term, former *New York Sun* and *Politico* editor Harry Siegel began writing pieces in the *Village Voice* that described how the mayor had cut down "what remained of working- and middle-class Manhattan. Gone, going, or forcibly shrinking are the Flower District, the Fur District, the Garment District, the Meatpacking District, and the Fulton Fish Market. Even the Diamond District is being nudged out of its 47th Street storefronts and into a city-subsidized new office tower."[43]

It wasn't only Manhattan that Mike set about "rebuilding." So many working- and middle-class neighborhoods have been bulldozed that the National Trust for Historic Preservation named New York the "teardown capital of the United States." The Trust found 18 communities in Queens, Staten Island, Brooklyn, and the Bronx where older homes were being destroyed for apartment buildings, upscale townhouses, and garish mansions.[44] The flood of new luxury developments drove out local residents, overcrowded the schools, and destroyed the character of these communities forever.

Unless you lived in one of the torn-up neighborhoods or owned one of those small businesses, you weren't likely to have cared or even heard about them. A handful of columnists and investigative reporters were on to Mike almost from the beginning, but the steady flow of positive coverage, and Mike's army of publicists who pumped out bogus statistics and flamboyant success stories, drowned out their voices. Even some who were troubled by the racial implications of his policies failed to grasp that the outcomes were precisely what he intended:

> *During Bloomberg's mayoralty, more and more poor people of color are being pushed out of Williamsburg, the Lower East Side, Harlem, Bushwick, Fort Greene, even Park Slope, and all the new housing is being placed in hyper-segregated neighborhoods. I think the big problem under Bloomberg is the re-segregation of the city by letting the market do its work without any sort of plan.*[45]

But Mike did have a plan.

> *We're the financial capital of the world. We need people who can afford to live here, eat in the restaurants, buy the season boxes, and shop at Bergdorf's. We're the glitziest, where-it's-happening place, we're gonna have the brand-new sports stadiums. This is Luxury City! Our city! Write that down.*

A Race to the Top

If you didn't think too much about it, his plan made sense. It's true that New York City isn't a low-cost place to do business. The race to the bottom run by many governments here and abroad, *Set up right here in [fill in the blanks]—we'll give you cheap land, no unions, no taxes, no health, safety, labor, or any other stinkin' regulations. C'mon down,* wouldn't work for New York.

As Mike put it, "To capitalize on our strengths, we'll continue to transform New York physically ... to make it even more attractive to the world's most talented people ... New York is the city where the world's best and brightest want to live and work."

Financial services, media, and information technology professionals are for the most part well-educated white people. They would be attracted to the city so long as they perceived it to be safe, clean, and in Mike's words, a "glitzy, happening place." And the businesses that employed them would want to be here too.

He recruited Dan Doctoroff as his chief deputy. A former Lehman Brothers banker who grew up in the suburbs of Detroit, Doctoroff is a multimillionaire who managed money for Texas billionaires. Neither he nor Mike understood New York City as it is lived and experienced outside of a few Manhattan zip codes. But they took over its government, commissioned a McKinsey management study, and began remaking the city as they thought it should be.

In a recent book, Dr. Julian Brash put it this way:

> *What the post-industrial elites that populated the highest levels of the administration described using the humble language of "public service" and "giving back" was in fact an assertion of their rightful place as the rulers of the city, an audacious and deeply political act ... the class-inflected imagining of New York as a place of competition, innovation, and cosmopolitanism that drew the "best and brightest" from around the globe. This inspired the city's campaign to rebrand the city as a luxury product ...* [46]

The developers and the Wall Street firms have been given extraordinarily large public subsidies and tax advantages that are locked in place for years through so-called PILOTS (Payments in Lieu of Taxes), contracts that cannot be overturned by future legislatures. The claims of jobs created in exchange for subsidies granted have been wildly inflated, and the jobs that have been created are mostly low-paying service jobs.

In 2002, as Mike was quietly making his plans for Luxury City, our fight at Independence Plaza was about to take a new and nastier turn. The Tribeca real estate market was back in force. The brokers' offices were "galleries," their listings were "collections."

CHAPTER SIX

Landlords, Politicians,
and Other Scoundrels

◄◦►

Mike had been in office less than a year when I got a message on my answering machine: "This is Laurence Gluck. I'm under contract to buy Independence Plaza. Please call me to set up a meeting." Harold Cohn, who was in his eighties, had found a younger man eager to take Independence Plaza out of the Mitchell-Lama program.

On September 12, 2002, together with three other tenant board members, I went to Gluck's offices in Lower Manhattan. He was waiting for us with the real estate broker who had arranged the deal, a thin, elderly man wearing an undertaker-black suit. The broker assured us we were going to "love the improvements Mr. Gluck is going to make." We had no problem with the improvements; we knew he'd make them. Whether we would be around to see them was the question. The broker's unctuous tone is standard for New York landlords when dealing with rent-regulated tenants. Before reaching for the cudgel: hand out the crayons and coloring books. I can only speculate but it appears that they think tenants would be landlords if they weren't stupid.

Gluck was in his shirtsleeves, an assistant at his side. "Call me Larry," he said, shaking everyone's hand and ushering us into seats around a conference table. A short, thin, brown-haired, balding man with a neat little mustache, the darting eyes behind the tight smile had me thinking here is a man who has been looking for his opportunities from an early age. He had found one in us.

He picked away at a large bowl of fruit, wiping his chin with a paper napkin. "Well, as I said on the phone, I have a contract to buy Independence Plaza. I've filed the papers, and I expect to take title very soon. I wanted to tell you about my plans. I'm taking the development out of the Mitchell-Lama program and eventually going to market rents. I anticipate getting the approvals without much difficulty." It was all low key and very sunny.

Getting no reaction, he continued. "Of course, I realize how stressful this is to the tenants. I grew up in the Bronx. My family didn't have any money. I don't have to go to market rents immediately. Government vouchers will protect most tenants. This will be a smooth transition. We can do it by attrition. I'm going to invest a lot of money in capital improvements."

Still no reaction.

Gluck looked across the table. "Some fruit, a Coke?"

"No thanks."

"Do you have any questions?"

"We're just here to listen," I said.

One of our board members asked, "Can we see the papers?"

"I'm afraid those are confidential."

"How much did you pay?" I asked.

"That's confidential too. But you can get whatever is on file at HPD."[48]

We knew all we needed to know. This was the fight we had been warning our neighbors about for two years.

We called a general tenant meeting. On the night of the meeting, as I hurried along the sidewalk, my head down, thinking about what I was going to say, I came upon an elderly couple walking very slowly just ahead. The man was wearing a brown suit, a white shirt, and a bow tie. He was holding his wife's arm at the elbow. A strikingly dignified black couple, they looked to be in their eighties. As I passed alongside, the man said, "Hello, Mr. Fabricant." It took me by surprise. I didn't know them and hadn't seen them in the neighborhood. I would have remembered.

I slowed down, said hello, and started forward again. The man gently touched my arm. I slowed down again. He said they had lived at Independence Plaza for many years and were worried about what was going to happen to them. "We don't have a lot of money," he said.

"I don't know where we'd go," his wife said, leaning forward across his body, expecting an answer.

"Don't worry. Nobody's getting kicked out," I replied with more confidence than I felt. What else could I say?

"I know you've got to get over to the meeting," he said. "We'll see you over there."

They both wished me luck and told me how much confidence they had in me. It was devastating.

I had retired as the president of a graduate school. When I was elected president of the tenant association, I'd wisecracked to my wife, "Now you can call me the president of small things." The encounter with that couple brought home to me in a way that the meeting with Gluck hadn't that this was no small thing.

--◄o►--

Tenants needed political help. Democratic politicians wanted to be known as tenant advocates, but they also wanted the real estate money. They couldn't fool the landlords and developers or their lawyers and lobbyists, but they could fool the tenants, so they did. They marched and rallied with the tenants. They shook their fists at Albany Republicans. They arranged meetings with other Democratic politicians and housing regulators; they passed resolutions, issued proclamations, held countless legislative hearings, and even introduced tenant-protection bills. Space prevents me from describing all the flummery and fakery, but here are a few examples.

A veteran city council member lived at Independence Plaza. She was term limited and off the public payroll for the first time in years. She told tenants she was going to Albany to meet with our state senator. Together they would draft a tenant-protection bill. She urged me to focus our efforts on helping her get the bill passed in Albany.

The senator and the council member knew as I did that no such law would ever come out of Albany. I was certain she was trying to get on his payroll. We were a large constituency. If she could convince him that the tenants, her neighbors, would follow her lead, he'd hire her and rid himself of a potential challenger; not a bad strategy for them, but it had nothing to do with helping us. When I told that to a board member, a long-time friend of the council member, she thought me too cynical. A few weeks later, the council member was on the Senate payroll working on a tenant-protection bill. She had one of the Senate Democrat lawyers call me for my "input." Eventually, she landed a minor judgeship and moved out of Independence Plaza.

Her successor was an affable lawyer who had mastered the art of the lesser politician: an earnest manner that implied total commitment to his constituents. Our cause, whatever it might be, was his cause. Service to it embodied the very purpose to which he had dedicated his professional life. Rhetorical clouds of civic virtue seemed to billow around his head.

He spoke of fearsome negotiations with higher-level officials. He issued press releases, wrote letters to the tenants, posed for pictures in the local papers. Had we asked, he would have promoted a City Council resolution calling for the mayor to preserve Mitchell-Lama housing, issue a proclamation of "Mitchell-Lama Day in New York." He would have written forceful letters on our behalf to the governor and the mayor; meetings, letters, resolutions, hearings—standard meaningless gestures.

Legislative resolutions have no legal significance. They are designed not to fix problems, but to show that the sponsoring politicians care. The meaningless gesture in all its manifestations is one of the great political art forms.

Commitments were surrounded by contingencies. The tenants heard the commitments. I heard the contingencies. The lawyer-politician hinted at a successful outcome, but only if we followed his leadership. Many tenants believed in him. I knew he would take us right off a cliff. Higher politicians and the housing bureaucracy encouraged his approach. They and he viewed the tenants through the same prism: We were outsiders, disturbers of the political peace.

Insider Perspective: City Agencies and Politicians

This is the place in my story that I have to dig a little deeper into the ways of New York politicians and bureaucrats to give the reader some insight into the mechanisms that enable—no, encourage—politicians to lie to their constituents. Whether we will be able to fix our broken political system remains to be seen, but it isn't possible unless people understand when and how they are being lied to.

I had been chief counsel to the city's Environmental Protection Administration, one of Mayor John Lindsay's superagencies made up of previously independent fiefdoms—the sanitation, air, and water resources departments. EPA was a large bureaucracy with a large, powerful, and politically active union—the sanitation workers. All elected officials want the political support of the city's unions. It's the main collective bargaining leverage that unions have. Every mayoral administration is different, but some things are constant.

City agencies are political players in their own spheres. Rank-and-file city council members, state legislators, even US senators and congressmen have less influence over them than one would think. They work for the mayor and are responsive to him and his political appointees.

The sources of power vary with each agency, but the authority to award contracts, deliver services, approve or deny licenses, advance or slow projects, hire and fire, dispense cash—some combination of these powers and others—accrues to all bureaucracies. Other sources of power are less visible.

Agencies collect, store, analyze, and disseminate information. Even officials in the same mayoral administration don't have easy access to agency databases. Statistical studies and methodologies have the sound and feel of scientific objectivity, but results are easily manipulated to rationalize political objectives. Does the mayor want to cut expenses by getting rid of a hospital that serves as the only medical facility for a few hundred thousand poor people in a congressional district without doctors or pharmacists? The relevant agency can do a bed-utilization study, conclude that the hospital isn't cost-effective, and recommend closing it down. The agency's public relations staff pumps and spins the administration's "on the merits" position. The people who are protesting and the politicians who are leading them are being "political."

Does an electric utility want to build a power plant in a densely populated neighborhood over the objections of the residents? The economic development agency may approve, but the environmental agency may resist.

Utility lobbyists will make their case to the agencies. If they fail to dislodge the necessary approvals, the utility's CEO will meet directly with the mayor. Access won't be a problem. The city's newspapers are likely to support the utility. The mayor will be warned that if he doesn't approve the plant the next blackout will be on him; this despite the fact that even if approved, the proposed plant wouldn't come on stream for years. To drive home the city's dependence on the utility, it even may slow the subways to a crawl during a heat wave, claiming an inability to meet peak energy demand on the system. All this actually occurred during Con Edison's fight to pressure John Lindsay to override EPA's refusal to approve its proposal to build a 1600-MW fossil fuel plant in Astoria Queens. Following a subway slowdown in the middle of a heat wave, I sat across from Lindsay and Charles Luce, Con Ed's chairman, and told Lindsay that the Federal Power Commission had advised me that Con Ed had sufficient reserves to keep the subways running at normal speed. There had been no need to slow down the trains. It was a political act. Whereupon Lindsay turned to Luce and said, "Chuck, I think you ought to keep the subways running tomorrow." Citizens who opposed the plant had little access and no chance to impact the decision or contest it once it was made. In all such cases where they aren't organized as a single-issue voting block, their access is almost certain to be cosmetic. Lindsay cut the baby in half and approved an 800-MW plant: a political act.

Agency decisions are rarely overturned in court. Well-established law proscribes judicial intervention in all but the most egregious cases. Thus, except for the mayors to whom they report—and not always them—judges and politicians have surprisingly little influence over bureaucrats. As for the housing bureaucrats—especially in New York—many of them, especially those at the higher levels, want to work in the real estate industry they regulate: Landlords and developers are career opportunities; tenants are problems.

Bureaucracies need take seriously only the most senior politicians, but even they need the bureaucrats for small favors. Are constituents complaining about infrequent garbage collections or, as in our case, demanding oversight of their landlord? The local legislator can't even get the sanitation or housing commissioner on the phone. There are 51 New York city council members, 86 assembly members, 36 state senators, and 29 congressmen who represent various districts in New York City. There is only one sanitation commissioner. The politician will have to ask for help from an assistant commissioner or someone lower on the food chain. If the agency doesn't respond, what can the politician do about it? Hold a hearing? Call a press conference? Complain to the mayor? Pass a bill? Not likely.

In city government where the sanitation workers pick up the garbage and remove the snow—or don't—union leaders and commissioners are far more important than local politicians. The latter can do little political damage; an incompetent sanitation commissioner or an aggressive union leader can be ruinous.

Understandably, therefore, local politicians try to maintain good working relationships with the bureaucrats. These politicians don't have much power, but they don't want their constituents to know that. Thus they tend to fulminate publicly against agency decisions but more often act as gatekeepers between the bureaucrats and their own constituents; hence the meaningless gesture. Often they will put a local activist on their payrolls, as our state senator and councilman did, to act as a buffer between the politician and the constituents. The person who signs the paycheck generally has the attention and loyalty of the person who cashes it.

The legislative leaders are in a different position. Schools, hospitals, libraries, dozens of interest groups in every political district want government help. Lesser politicians must appear responsive, but as mentioned they can satisfy only a very few demands. And they mustn't make too many demands on the leaders who can actually do something. These few have many mouths to feed, not only the constituents in their own districts but all the other politicians, financial supporters, and interest groups, particularly the real estate lobby. The lesser politician who publicly criticizes his own party leader on behalf of his constituents or resists party discipline where discipline is expected puts in jeopardy his own position.

Those in good standing with the leadership are given discretionary, unaudited cash to spread around to organized groups in their districts. Sometimes these groups employ family members of the legislative sponsor. The cash payments may be known as member items, earmarks, or 007s, signifying that neither the sponsor's identity nor the money's purposes are open to public scrutiny, often not disclosed to anyone but the leader and a handful of other insiders on a need-to-know basis. (In a recent scandal, Christine Quinn, the current city council speaker, was caught funnelling money to groups that didn't exist.) Tenants, of course, rarely know about the existence of these funds, let alone how to get at them. The leaders also dispense lulus, payments in lieu of expenses awarded for "extra" legislative duties such as committee chairmanships or meaningless titled positions.

With such little leverage on the executive branch or their own party leaders, local politicians hoard their modest political capital and, if possible, put their constituents to sleep. Politicians, bureaucrats, landlords, developers, and lobbyists understand all this. They live in the same world. Only the constituents are ignorant.

In trying to explain to tenants how they were being manipulated, I sometimes felt as though I were deprogramming the victims of a cult. Until they realized that "the powers that be" weren't on their side, some tenants resented me. People tend to believe their local politicians. They believed especially in C. Virginia Fields, a black woman of humble origins who had become the Manhattan borough president, a position without substance whose holder is concerned with one thing: getting to the next rung on the political ladder, especially when the one s/he occupies is insecure, made so by term limits.

In 1999, Fields established a Mitchell-Lama Task Force, promoting it as a tenant advocacy group and herself as the city's leading tenant advocate. The task force met each month in her offices. Sitting around a large conference table, the tenant leaders were served bagels and coffee, donuts, and soft drinks. Strategies were discussed, agendas prepared, and resolutions drafted. Issues were debated, memoranda were produced and revised. But the task force never actually did anything.

I felt obligated to attend a few of these meetings until I could bear it no longer. By the time I quit going, some 47 Mitchell-Lama developments had been deregulated, and the rents driven up. This, after all, was why the owners were exiting the program. Many of the tenant presidents who attended the meetings were gone.

In 2005, the real estate lobby financed Fields' Democratic primary race for mayor. She finished far behind. Now there is another borough president. You can see the new man's name on a sign as you come over the Brooklyn Bridge. The task force continues to meet under his auspices. He is thought to be a tenant advocate. Rumor has it he is planning to run for citywide office.

—◄o►—

Busloads of tenants go to Albany each year. Virginia Fields paid for the buses. There, in the Legislative Office Building, prominent Democrats made fiery speeches urging tenants to press the Republican-controlled Senate to pass the tenant-protection bills that they had passed in the Democratic-controlled Assembly. These bills are known as "one-house" bills. Essentially, they are press releases meant to demonstrate fealty to the tenants' cause, not to become laws. I have heard it said that lobbyists have legislators introduce one-house bills on various subjects so that they can be retained to support or defeat them. With, for example, Atlantic City casino owners paying lobbyists to prevent gambling casinos from opening in New York, and upstate hotel interests paying lobbyists to advance the idea of opening such casinos, the money is good on both sides and nobody has to leave the office. Whether such stories are apocryphal I can't say; that they are widely believed tells you something about the political culture.

—◄o►—

On one Albany Mitchell-Lama day, I watched the chair of the Assembly housing committee, Vito Lopez, who has made a specialty of one-house, pro-tenant bills, present an award to a veteran tenant advocate for "all that you have done for tenants." The octogenarian had been coming to Albany for years, but had won nothing from the legislature. Lopez was giving him the award to associate himself with the tenants' cause, not to advance it. The advocate trudged up onto the stage to accept the award. The hundreds of Mitchell-Lama tenants in the hearing room clapped and cheered. I sat in that audience almost embarrassed to be there. I had brought some Independence Plaza tenants with me but had told them not to expect anything. We were just there to support the cause.

Lopez has since been caught up in a scandal involving the funnelling of millions of dollars to a senior-citizen complex in his district where his long-time girlfriend is paid hundreds of thousands of dollars a year to do something for seniors. It may all be legal. Not for nothing are legislators called lawmakers. Lopez continues to hold legislative hearings on affordable housing.

Lopez follows in a long tradition. The Legislative Office Building in Albany is one of a complex of government buildings officially called the Nelson Rockefeller Empire State Plaza.

The complex is its own monument to political bullshit and one of the more entertaining examples of how it can sometimes soar to—one hesitates to say it— poetic heights.

The building project would take eighteen years to complete and cost more than $2 billion. Not even Nelson Rockefeller could have sold it to the voters, so he didn't ask them.

First, he established the "Temporary State Commission on the Capital City," chaired by his faithful Lieutenant Governor, Malcolm Wilson. The commission concluded that Albany required "a Capital City for New York State second to none in our nation—or indeed, in the world."

Second, the Commission recommended a site that comprised 29 blocks and parts of 11 more. An estimated 7,000 people lived there. There were two public schools and about 350 small businesses. That was the site Rockefeller wanted.

In 1962, the Rockefeller-dominated legislature voted $20 million to acquire all the land and buildings on the 98.5 acres. (Rockefeller low-balled the projected costs, claiming it could be completed for $250 million.)

Next, he flattened the entire neighborhood. Brute physical and political force evicted everyone and everything from the site. It was all legal.

Here's the creative part. The Nelson Rockefeller Empire State Plaza was financed through a lease-purchase agreement. The law allowed municipalities to issue bonds in excess of their legal debt limits without voter approval, provided the bonds were self-liquidating. Enter Albany's legendary mayor, Erastus Corning, a Democrat and the nation's longest-serving mayor.

The City of Albany issued a series of 40-year self-liquidating municipal bonds and the state became the contractor for what, according to the legal documents, was a city project. The state would take legal title to the state capital buildings only when the bonds were fully amortized 40 years later. Meanwhile, the state would pay rent to the city in amounts sufficient to liquidate the debt. State voters don't get to vote on contracts or rental agreements. Because the bonds were issued by the city and were self-liquidating through the state rental payments, the city could issue them without voter approval. Only Rockefeller and Corning had to sign off.

Before they cut the deal, Corning had called the proposal "a ruthless takeover." He accused Rockefeller of "planning to carve out from the heart of the city a large, sterile area for a monumental group of buildings which will look most spectacular on postcards but will, in fact, hurt the people of Albany." Albany Democrats called it "hasty and ruthless ... what might be expected in a dictatorship."

After the deal was cut, in Corning's words, the project became "a living monument, a place for pleasure as well as work, a place for homes and music and beauty and culture as well as the most spectacular complex of government offices ever dreamed of."

What could have caused this paean to the virtues of a project that earlier had been so vehemently condemned? Polly Noonan, Corning's long-time companion, owned the privately held insurance company that insured the complex. Rockefeller chose the National Commercial Bank and Trust Company of Albany as the depository for cash proceeds of his various bond sales. About $1 billion flowed through the bank as a consequence. Corning was a major stockholder in the bank.

The State Bank of Albany processed the state's rental payments to the county. Corning, and his mother and father, were directors of that bank. Corning was also the president of Albany Associates, Inc., the insurance and brokerage firm that insured contractors on the project.[49]

—◄o►—

I returned from Albany Mitchell-Lama Day as dispirited as ever. I was desperate to change the battleground from law to politics and the venue from Albany to New York City, where I felt we might be able to bring some pressure to bear on Bloomberg. By now, I was beginning to understand the mayor's character and agenda. We had

5,000 postcards printed up and distributed to tenants around the city to be mailed to Michael Bloomberg and Sheldon Silver, the Assembly Speaker.

Mike was not yet fully engaged in his *greatest-affordable-housing-program* razzle. He simply ignored us. But Silver's director of "constituent services" called me. "Why is Speaker Silver getting all these postcards? He doesn't represent you."

"He's the speaker, isn't he?"

"Independence Plaza isn't in his district. Your assemblywoman is Deborah Glick. We've forwarded all these postcards to her. Please don't send us any more cards."

I already knew there would be no Albany legislation to help tenants. I thought Deborah Glick might be persuaded to intercede with Silver. He was the most powerful Democrat in the state. All he had to do was pick up the phone and call Bloomberg.

I had no illusions. Glick had sent the tenants a letter that proclaimed her concern for affordable housing generally and Independence Plaza in particular. She enclosed a copy of the letter she had sent to Deputy Mayor Dan Doctoroff, urging him to help us. Constituents who receive copies of such letters think they mean: *I'm working hard on your behalf.* For the recipient, what they signal is: *This is what I have to do to get them off my back. You can ignore this letter.* A serious effort would require a closed-door meeting, an alternative proposal, and a phone call from the Assembly speaker to the mayor or his chief deputy asking that something be done. It irritated me that Glick was giving tenants the crayons and coloring book treatment. Her letter was just a variation of the one-house bill.

Having in mind the truth of Professor Frankfurt's statement that "most people think they can recognize bullshit when they see it, but often they can't," it's worthwhile to highlight this political ploy because it's used in so many different contexts. When, for example, politicians agree that banks need to be more tightly regulated but then say that in this globalized economy it can't be done unless other countries tighten their regulations, think of it as a variation of the one-house bill, especially when it's a bank-financed politician who's saying it. That there may be a germ of truth in it makes it that much more convincing.

In December 2002, we published in a local newspaper a two-page letter of our own, addressed to Mayor Bloomberg. We delivered a copy to his office. We pointed to the history of corrupt management at many Mitchell-Lama developments and recounted his housing agency's refusal to act. Why not preserve the affordable housing that exists when it costs so much more to replace it? Mike ignored us.

We published another letter, this one addressed to Silver, whose district was adjacent to ours. We placed it in the same paper in which he ran a weekly advertisement that included his photograph and cited his advocacy for tenants. We said:

We are your next-door neighbors, several thousand working-class people who live in Independence Plaza, just north of Ground Zero. ... We are making this public appeal because we haven't been able to get through to you ... We think the mayor and his deputy would help us, if only you conveyed to them how important this issue is to you.

Shortly thereafter, Deborah Glick called to say that she had arranged a meeting with Silver in his offices in Lower Manhattan. As we sat on the couch in his outer office, she asked, "What are you going to ask the speaker to do?"

"I want him to call Bloomberg or Doctoroff and let them know that he wants something done to protect Independence Plaza tenants."

Glick nodded. She had no problem with that. We had already talked about it on the phone. I had a Plan B but before we finished our conversation, we were called into the meeting. Silver was sitting to my left at the end of a long conference table. Glick sat between us. Silver's chief of staff was across from me, a glowering presence. I thanked him for meeting with me.

"It isn't your meeting; it's Deborah Glick's meeting," he said.

I knew then that this was only a courtesy meeting; the kind granted to favored lobbyists. The client is impressed that the lobbyist has arranged it and doesn't know that he's playing a bit part in a piece of political theater. Think of Jack Abramoff bringing in his Indian chief clients to see George Bush and Tom DeLay. The Indian tribes had paid Abramoff millions of dollars. How that money was divided probably will never be known, but in this instance I was the Indian chief, and I hadn't even paid for the meeting. Nothing would come of it.

Silver asked, "What do you want me to do?"

"I want you to call Doctoroff and tell him you'd like something done to help the tenants at Independence Plaza."

Presumably, Glick had already told him what we wanted when she arranged the meeting. He said he'd make the call, but "if Doctoroff has made up his mind, I won't be able to change it." This, everyone in the room knew, was a modest assessment of his leverage. Mike had been courting him from the day he took office. He needed Silver to advance his agenda.

Ironically, because the Speaker is so powerful, a fact lamented by good government groups, Silver was one of the few people in the state who could say no to Mike. Whatever powers state government had in relation to the city and whatever powers the state legislature had in relation to the state government were held by two men; one of them was Sheldon Silver. That, I think, is worth explaining. I have limited experience outside of New York politics, but I'm confident that similar dynamics apply to many other legislative bodies throughout the nation, though people do say Albany is a special case.

INSIDER PERSPECTIVE: ALBANY

The adjective "dysfunctional" is permanently affixed to the New York State Legislature. Accounts of three men in a room—the governor, speaker, and majority leader—who decide everything is accurate, if vastly oversimplified.

Everything government deals with—housing, health, banking, energy, education, and so forth—engages the close attention of thousands of people. Banks, insurance companies, hospitals, trial lawyers, doctors, beer and wine distributors, teachers, healthcare workers, real estate developers—all the important interests in the state—maintain lobbying operations in Albany, as do colleges and universities, county governments, and non-profit groups of every description, including New York City.

The Policy Networks

Think of each such interest as being represented within an informal network that includes, say, the committee chairmen in each legislative chamber, the relevant state commissioner, high-level legislative and executive staff, lobbyists, the heads of trade associations, and many other private and public players.

So, for example, colleges and universities might be thought of as part of the higher education network, banks as part of the banking network. The members of each such network have common, conflicting, and overlapping interests. There are savings banks, community banks, and commercial banks in the banking network, and there are private and public colleges in the higher education network. As a general rule, nothing of any significance moves in Albany without the members of the relevant policy network being aware of it. Depending on whether and how an issue impacts them, they will ignore it or try to advance, oppose, or modify it. Likely one of the private sector interests has initiated it. Politics is a reactive business. Mike is an exception.

These private interests combine in trade associations that are usually headed by former government officials. The associations draft, introduce, and track legislation and regulations, they testify before committees, serve as job clearing houses, contribute money, and in general stay on top of everything that impacts their members.

The largest interests, say a major commercial bank, have their own lobbyists who pursue agendas outside of the common interests of their trade associations. These lobbyists may be employees who hold titles such as "vice-president for government relations." or they may be contract lobbyists—the law and lobbying firms who populate every large state and city capital and Washington.

The lobbyists generally have close relationships with at least one of the three men in the room or at least with those who influence them. They raise political money from their clients and give it to politicians. A lobbyist with a large list of clients may be lobbying on a particular issue for a given client, but the fact that the lobbyist represents many other contributors won't be lost on the politician.

Albany is a community whose members interact socially and professionally within a small geographic area. They have a finely calibrated sense of the power, leverage, and character of the people they deal with. It's a common mistake, one that the smartest tenants made, to think that enlisting the support of, say, the head of the teachers' union would advance the tenants' cause. It wasn't worth the effort. The union head would have little leverage on the outcome of our fight, if only because the insiders would understand that the union leader wouldn't spend much time or political capital on things that didn't affect her members directly. She was an important player in shaping education policy, but she wasn't part of the housing/real estate network.

As with city council members, few state legislators have meaningful power or more than modest decision-making influence, far less than the top staff people who work for one of the three men in the room. With few exceptions state legislators are foot soldiers. As with city council members, one of their main functions is to keep their constituents away from the real decision-makers.

Eric Lane, former counsel to the Democratic Senate minority and a law professor at Hofstra University, put it this way:

> *Yes, New Yorkers cast their votes for State Assembly and Senate, but when the vast majority of their representatives arrive at the Capitol, they don't legislate; they meekly follow the instructions of their legislative leaders. It is no exaggeration to say that the speaker of the Assembly and the majority leader of the Senate are the legislative branch in Albany. They pick the issues, close the deals, and—ultimately—make the laws.*[50]

The speaker and majority leader oversee their own legislative party political operations. They may select candidates, distribute campaign money, and even oversee field operations that local parties once performed. Lobbyists give money to the campaign committees that the leaders redistribute to individual members. They also direct the distribution of state (and public authority) money, often to legislators who are running in the few pieces of political geography that haven't been made safe for one party or the other through the reapportionment process. For the most important objective of any legislative party is to gain and hold the majority; the minority gets table scraps. Because congressional and legislative districts are redrawn every ten years, the individual legislator's political career, including the state's congressmen, is in the leader's hands.

Committee assignments and chairmanships, professional staff, the flow of legislation, compensation beyond the statutory pay scale—all are within the leader's discretion. Even office space, equipment, and personnel might go through the leader. The list goes on.

His political power extends beyond the legislature to judgeships, nominations for various offices, and leverage over business interests in a local legislator's district. Generally, once the leader is chosen by the members of his own party, he accumulates too much power to be challenged. He serves until he dies or retires. His ability to reward and punish his members, his leverage over lobbyists, business interests, labor unions, politicians outside the legislature, and all the rest of it are too much to resist.

Those who seek and fail to topple a leader, something rarely attempted, are quickly stripped of their legislative positions and whatever other benefits they enjoy. They're lucky if their seats in the legislative chamber aren't physically removed. Despite calls for reform and some cosmetic changes, virtually everything the legislative leader wants to control in his own legislative chamber, he does. Voters generally don't understand that the vote that counts is the vote to organize the legislative chamber. A vote for a liberal Republican over a conservative Democrat is a vote for Republican legislative control.

Local elections that emphasize the voting records and character of the candidates rather than their party affiliations are therefore misleading, often deliberately so. When, for example, a Republican state senator carved out a reputation as tenant-friendly, it was because his district contained many rent-regulated developments. He was allowed off the Republican reservation to introduce meaningless legislation for tenants so as to keep the district in Republican hands and thus contribute to the Republican senate majority, which would kill the tenant legislation. A tenant advocate chastised me one day in Albany for suggesting to the senator's chief of staff that it made no sense for tenants to support him. She, the tenant advocate, didn't get it: The senator always introduced strong tenant legislation and returned her phone calls.

Again, Sheldon Silver only had to pick up the phone for us and indicate he was serious. Bloomberg needed Silver's support for virtually everything he wanted to accomplish. Silver's authority cut across all the policy networks. With Pataki and Bruno (the Republican Senate majority leader) more or less in the Bloomberg bag, Silver was the only politician he had to worry about.

The Staffs

The big decisions, those that involve large numbers of people and dollars, directly involve the governor and the two legislative leaders, hence the idea of three (white) men in a room. Neither a woman nor a black person has ever held any of these positions. But by the time something important works its way into that room, the top staff aides have sifted through the political, policy, money, and personal issues and narrowed the options.

These top aides carry broad portfolios and hold various titles. They include the secretary to the governor, chief counsel, budget director, maybe the press officer, the directors of the finance and ways and means committees, and a few others. The power that each aide enjoys depends on his or her relationship with the elected official who appointed him. Everyone who does serious business knows who the real players are. They are in constant negotiation, not only with their counterparts in the other party, but more often with players in their own party and lobbyists for various interests.

If you were to walk into the office of the secretary to the governor, for example, the top staff person, you might see a half-dozen buttons on the telephone lit up, blinking away as important players around the state queue up to speak for a minute or two. The callers who get through aren't schmoozing; they're doing business. The secretary transcends the policy networks.

Academic models don't offer much insight into this system. In this—and I say it respectfully—they can be likened to travel guides that describe the museums, restaurants, hotels, and landmarks, calculate the distances, schedules, and modes of transportation, and sometimes offer an account of an area's history to suggest how it got to be the place it is today. They may have much to offer the traveller who plans to spend days or even weeks in an unfamiliar place. But doing business in a foreign country requires a deeper understanding of the culture, the mores, and the players. People who invest their money or who have serious political problems understand the need for an insider who can represent them. It's not the local legislator.

Silver's comment that this was Glick's meeting, not mine and that if Doctoroff said no, there was nothing he could do simply reinforced the message: *No help here.*

I put Plan B on the table. "Well, if we can't move Doctoroff, suppose we can get the Senate to agree to a rent-stabilization bill that protects just Ground Zero tenants, say everything south of Fourteenth Street?"

For years, the Democrats had proclaimed their concern for tenants, knowing that the Republican-controlled Senate would kill anything they passed in the Assembly. If the Senate Republicans actually passed a bill, I thought, it might be awkward for Silver to kill it.

A funereal silence settled over the room. Silver glanced at Glick. She hadn't prepared him for that.

"What you're asking the speaker to do is unfair," she jumped in. "He has many members with Mitchell-Lamas in their districts. He can't give you special consideration." We were her constituents. She was making it clear that this wasn't her idea.

"You get Bruno to pass a bill, and we'll see about it," Silver said.

—◄o►—

Something that had happened to me in Albany years earlier had given me the Ground Zero idea. As it's a concrete illustration of how things work, I'll tell the story briefly. It was the late 1980s and I was seeking legislative funding for the graduate school I had organized. A powerful Republican friend asked the staff director of the Republican-controlled Senate Finance Committee to advance the funding, provided that the Assembly Democrats demanded nothing in return from the Republican budget negotiator. If the two legislative negotiators agreed, the governor's higher education budget official would sign off on the deal.

The Senate finance director instructed his higher education budget negotiator to advance the funding request, but if the Democratic negotiator asked for anything in return, to take it off the table, as he was only advancing it as a favor to my friend.

I arranged the same commitment on the Democratic side; namely, that if the Senate advanced the funding proposal, the Democratic negotiator would not ask for anything in return. Given the size of the state budget, the modest request—I don't recall the number, maybe $150,000—wasn't even a footnote in the education budget. It would be regarded as a no-cost item, that is, it wouldn't be "charged" to either party. The money was important, but just as important was that insiders would know the school had enough political support to be included in the budget.

Gubernatorial and legislative staffs often have their own agendas. If they can leave no footprints while pursuing them, even against the wishes of their principals, they sometimes do.

The Senate negotiator, who didn't like the idea, advanced it by saying to the Ways and Means negotiator, "This guy wants his own graduate school." The Democrat, a friend who had been forewarned, understood what her opposite number was up to—he wanted her to reject his request or ask for a quid pro quo so that he could follow the letter, if not the spirit, of his instructions, and take the funding off the table.

"Maybe we should give it to him," she replied. He had to agree and move on. The money was in the budget. It was that incident that had given me the idea to try to advance a tenant bill through a Republican initiative.

Everything would depend on persuading Joe Bruno, the Senate majority leader, to pass the Ground Zero bill first in the Senate. I had talked it over with a partner in the law firm that represented us. He had run for statewide office on the Republican ticket. He thought he could persuade Bruno.

I knew I might have to raise some political money from tenants, but without Silver's prior commitment I couldn't ask tenants to contribute more than they already had, money most of them couldn't afford. At best, it was a long shot, probably a dumb idea. We'd be better off saving our money for a New York City effort.

As we left Silver's office, his assistant snarled, "We didn't appreciate the letter you published in the *Downtown Express*." "I've been around Albany for a long time," I said. "I know better than to piss off the speaker, but we're trying to save our homes and we couldn't even get a meeting."

Silver watched the exchange with a sort of reptilian calm. He didn't say anything. Glick assured me she would follow up on the phone call to Doctoroff. I knew she wouldn't, and I never heard from her or Silver again.

If the tenants were going to get help keeping their homes, it would have to come from the man all landlords and developers deferred to: Mike, not yet the Affordable Housing Mayor.

◄○►

We finally got a meeting with Dan Doctoroff. He had promised not to approve the sale from Cohn to Gluck until we could present our case. A few days before the meeting, he called me to say that he had approved the sale. We could have our meeting, though.

I decided to go ahead with it. The case we made boiled down to this: Why should you allow Gluck to buy up the property, walk off with millions, and put 3,500 people in perpetual fear of losing their homes and many actually losing them? Why eliminate the city's most important affordable housing stock? Tribeca doesn't need another luxury real estate development. The taxpayers paid for everything in the first place. Gluck isn't a stakeholder in any sense of the word. Neither Cohn nor Gluck invested much, if anything, or took any risks. Our plan gives Cohn rich profits, much more than we think he deserves.

Surrounded by his housing commissioners and deputies, Doctoroff lauded the administration's affordable-housing program and the regulatory zeal of his housing agency. He couldn't do anything for us. He said we should go and negotiate with Gluck, who personally had assured him he would be "fair." That assurance merely confirmed that Gluck had access to Bloomberg's top deputy. The tens of thousands of Mitchell-Lama tenants had to organize demonstrations, march, raise money, publish letters in the local newspapers—and even then all we could get was a pro forma meeting telling us the administration had already decided the issue. But there it was: We'd get no help from City Hall: Talk to Gluck. He'll be fair.

CHAPTER SEVEN

Feeding the
Beast

—◄o►—

Ve had been stonewalled across the board: the housing regulators, the state and city Democrats, and now, the top person in Bloomberg's administration. We were running out of options. Somehow we would have to get to Mike and put some pressure on him. First, we'd have to meet with Laurence Gluck. Now that Doctoroff had approved the sale, I had little hope that a meeting would get us anywhere.

Gluck: It's My Football Now

In July 2003, at our lawyers' offices, we had our first serious meeting with Gluck and his chief lawyer, Stephen Meister. They oozed confidence. The two of them sat across the table from me and the three lawyers on our side.

Gluck opened the meeting. "It's my football now," he said. He asked why other board members weren't there. Maybe he wondered whether I could deliver an agreement even if one were reached; or maybe he wanted to see whether he could exploit any divisions among the tenants. He had assured the many elderly tenants they had nothing to worry about. I had told them that if they got an enforceable agreement from him, I would apologize for what some perceived as my cynicism, not his. They never got the agreement.

"I'm representing the tenants. For now at least, I have the board's proxy."

"What do you propose?" Gluck asked.

"We want to buy you out. Give us a price," one of our lawyers responded.

"There is no price, I'm not selling."

"Independence Plaza doesn't have sentimental value for you. Surely there is a price at which you would sell," our lawyer replied.

"No, there isn't. I didn't buy it to flip it. I'm a long-term investor."

We had come to the first dead end.

"Let's talk about the tenants," I said. "What do you propose?"

"The vouchers will protect two-thirds of the tenants."

"That's what you say; but even if you're right, what about the others?"

"I'll treat them fairly."

Alan Epstein, our lead lawyer, pressed him. "If you're certain that the vouchers will be available to tenants, will you guarantee them?"

"No."

"So," Epstein said, "you want the tenants to guarantee them."

No response.

We knew he would never agree to a guarantee. We were getting nowhere.

We talked for a while, but it was just talk. Gluck was feeling things out. He wasn't about to agree to anything.

"Look," he said, "I don't blame you for fighting this. I would do the same."

"That's very generous of you," I replied. I was being sarcastic but he nodded, as though I had complimented him. One of our lawyers laughed out loud. Gluck was offended. We decided to take a break.

After the meeting, Alan Epstein told me that as he and Gluck were standing over adjoining urinals, Gluck said to him, "Your client hates me."

Epstein replied, "Hate is too strong; he's angry." It was a distinction without much of a difference; lawyers are good at that sort of thing.

When the meeting resumed, Gluck said, "You and I are just alike, you're trying to make as much money as you can"—he presumably meant I was trying to keep my rent as low as possible—"and I'm trying to be fair and make money too."

"You're terrorizing 3,500 people. I'm not."

He didn't say anything.

"What about the non-voucher tenants, what does 'fair' mean?" I asked. "Assuming there is no rent stabilization for Independence Plaza, they're completely unprotected."

"What do you propose?" Meister interjected. This is a standard negotiating ploy: The first person who puts the number on the table loses. Meister, I would learn, took great pride in being a wily negotiator.

"It isn't my place to propose anything. You've got the property, and you say you're going to exit Mitchell-Lama but you're going to be fair. What do you mean? I need to take an offer back to the board and the tenants."

Gluck turned to Meister. "He's right. I will make an offer in a month or so."

"I'll be leaving in a couple of weeks for Amsterdam," I told him, "but I'll be in touch with the lawyers. So, can we expect an offer by, say, September?"

Gluck agreed.

We had accomplished all that we could. The meeting ended. We never received an offer; Gluck disappeared. He had satisfied his obligation to meet with us. With his lobbyists and lawyers in contact with Doctoroff, the housing agency officials, and anyone else who counted, our fate would be decided behind closed doors. We weren't invited. *Not about us without us* isn't a slogan I invented, but it's a first principle of politics. If you're not in the room or aren't reliably represented, you're an outsider. If you're a rent-regulated tenant in Luxury City, you're screwed. We had one last move.

Our Strategy

City Council Speaker Gifford Miller was the one remaining politician who might be able to help. The council is a weak institution, but it had some leverage on Bloomberg. I decided to try to pass a bill in the city council. For that, we'd need a serious lobbyist.

I had known Ethan Geto casually for years. Six feet, six inches tall, stoop shoul-dered, in his sixties, he was a well-known gay activist who had begun his politi-cal life as a reformer. He was now a lobbyist for real estate developers. (A tenant advocate would later criticize me for retaining him. Not always, but too often, I found that advocates whose homes weren't at stake were easy to manipulate by politicians. The advocates wanted to think of themselves as insiders and always presented themselves as such to tenants.) I always thought of Ethan as an honest person; everyone has to pay the rent.

In this kind of insider politics, the "ask" is always the threshold issue. Many unwritten rules surround it: Don't ask for something the politician can't deliver, understand how much political capital he will have to spend to accommodate you, figure out what and who will induce him to spend it, and make it easy for him. Don't ask for two things, one that's crucial and one that's unimportant; you'll always get the latter. If you need a phone call, put the phone against his ear and dial the num-ber. There's more to it—cash, for one thing—but that's the general idea.

In addition to bundling real estate money, effective lobbyists are like cultural anthropologists: participant observers. They understand the political ledgers that poli-ticians carry around in their heads, the favors received and the due bills owed, the lever-age that the players have over one another, the personal quirks and the unarticulated protocols that govern every political culture. Ethan knew how things worked in New York City, and he knew the players. He had helped Miller become Speaker in a politi-cal fight that had been decided by one vote. (Ethan had bundled his clients' real estate money and given it to Miller, who in turn distributed it to selected candidates. When they won office, Miller collected on the due bills.) Ethan was in very good standing. Before he agreed to represent us, he'd have to see whether he had a conflict with any of his clients. Maybe, I thought, he'd speak to Miller first. I didn't know and didn't ask.

He gave me no guarantees, but if he didn't think we had a chance, I didn't think he'd take our money. Lobbyists aren't always that scrupulous. Miller was planning to run for mayor. Ethan was a source of real estate money and political advice. I didn't think Miller would lie to him.

I stated my expectations: "Ethan, my position is that Miller doesn't bullshit Ethan, and Ethan doesn't bullshit Neil, right?"

He agreed. A couple of weeks later, we shook hands on a deal.

The fee was $48,000: $15,000 as a retainer, the balance over a one-year period. Not a lot of money in New York's real estate/politics world. Donald Trump, for example, once circumvented campaign contribution limits by spreading $150,000 around among eighteen subsidiary companies.[51] That was the 1985 New York elec-tion cycle, 25 years earlier. Still, the fee was a lot of money for us. Ethan said he thought we were the good guys, which counted for something.

Over the next couple of weeks, we sat around with our lawyers developing a piece of legislation. It had to be strong enough to worry Mitchell-Lama owners, but not so strong that it overreached the city council's legal authority. Provided that a bill is legally defensible—and not always then—politics generally trumps law.

Our bill had two key elements. The first required landlords who wanted to exit the Mitchell-Lama program to pay a "community impact fee" to mitigate the damages suffered by the loss of affordable housing. Ethan's idea was to make it a flexible fee, based on the housing agency's findings. That would make it tougher for landlords to claim that the bill imposed so severe a financial burden that it effectively denied them the right to exit the program, something only Albany could do.

The second element required landlords to establish that their developments had been in substantial compliance with Mitchell-Lama's requirements. They had received the program's benefits, why shouldn't they have had to comply with its obligations? It would be a difficult hurdle, especially at Independence Plaza where top management had taken bribes from people to jump the waiting lists. (We didn't know how high up the money flowed. The assistant commissioner in charge of the Mitchell-Lama program said it didn't matter and the Department of Investigation refused our request to investigate.)

Finally, the bill provided that if landlords reached a negotiated agreement with tenants, the bill's provisions were waived; if not, they would have to satisfy its requirements or go to court to overturn it, a much tougher position than tenants going into court to fight a legally permissible exit from the program.

The bill wasn't a showstopper. Had it been, we wouldn't have been able to get it considered. The idea of a community impact fee came from a law review article sent to me by a pro bono lawyer. He had read the article and drafted a crude bill without a supporting memorandum. I asked him not to surface the proposal without first refining it and allowing us to develop the political muscle to back it up. He was inexperienced and politically ambitious. He went ahead anyway. He told me he had given it to Virginia Fields, the borough president. Reportedly, she passed it on to Miller's staff where it was rejected out of hand. We now had an added hurdle to overcome. We had gotten to "no" before we had a chance to present our strongest case, politically and on the merits.

Our purpose was to inject uncertainty into the buyout process and thus make Gluck's financing more difficult. All we wanted was a negotiation in which we had some leverage. By then, we knew Mike would veto it, but if we could get a veto-proof majority of the council, he'd have to swallow it. With Miller's support, we had a chance; without it, we had none. Ethan set up a meeting with Miller.

Miller Commits

After weeks of negotiations with Miller and his staff, we had an agreement on the wording of the bill that he would sponsor, and we had gathered enough commitments from the city council to secure a veto-proof majority. More weeks went by. Miller still hadn't introduced the bill. We learned that he was also meeting with Gluck and his lobbyists and lawyers. I was pretty sure he was using our bill to extract some real estate money from them. Ethan was still our only bridge to Miller. But the doors were closed, the money was on the table, and we weren't in the room. We had to do more.

We enlisted the support of the Working Families Party, a union-backed political party that had supplanted the Liberal Party as an important player in New York politics. Candidates, including Mike, wanted the WFP ballot line.[52]

With the help of Julie Miles, a political organizer whom we had hired and who had led the effort to secure the veto-proof majority in the city council, we organized a rally of tenants from Mitchell-Lama buildings all over the city for a day in June 2003. Ethan called to say that Miller wanted to speak.

"Ethan, we aren't going to bullshit each other, right? Why would we allow him to pose as a tenant advocate when he hasn't advanced our bill like he said he would?"

After a few phone calls back and forth, Ethan called to say it was a done deal. It was only the introduction of the bill, not its passage, but it would commit Miller publicly, and it was the first daylight we'd seen in more than two years. I agreed to let him talk at the rally.

The night of the meeting came. The 800-seat auditorium was packed with tenants from all over the city carrying cardboard signs that identified their developments. I introduced Miller to the crowd. He began to speak.

Straining to evoke a passion that plainly wasn't there, he talked about Ellis Island and the city of immigrants, the importance of affordable housing, and so on. Hollow phrases and stilted delivery—he was painful to listen to. Would we never encounter a politician who believed in what he was saying? What a terrible job, I thought, to go out night after night, feigning enthusiasm for things other people care about.

He droned on. Where was the commitment Ethan had promised?

Then our tenant vice-president began leading a chant: "Save our homes! Save our homes!"

Miller looked out at 800 chanting people holding up their cardboard signs and seemed to wake up. "I will push the legal envelope for you. We will soon introduce legislation to preserve the affordability of Mitchell-Lama apartments!"

The crowd exploded: "Miller for mayor!" He was beaming.

As he walked off the stage to more applause, Ethan, from behind the curtain, whispered to him, "Wave and smile." Miller's hand shot up. He smiled. Another whisper: "Neil, escort him off the stage!"

I took a few steps and stopped. Taking Ethan's stage directions was a step too far. I couldn't do it. Not much of a bottom line, I admit, but we finally had a public commitment from a politician who counted for something.

Miller scheduled a press conference and rally at City Hall, to be followed by an introduction of, and hearing on, the bill. We'd supply the bodies at the rally and the witnesses at the hearing.

Show Me the Money

Days before the city council hearing, Ethan called to invite me to a Miller for Mayor fundraiser at the home of Judith and Robert Rubin. Months earlier, I had volunteered that I would try to raise some campaign money—not anywhere near as much as the real estate crowd, of course, but maybe enough for Miller to notice. It was time to make good on the commitment.

I phoned twenty Independence Plaza tenants and asked each of them to contribute $250. The New York City campaign finance law gave candidates four-to-one matching funds for contributions up to $250, thus we would be giving what amounted to a $20,000 contribution. This fight had forced me into all sorts of uncomfortable situations. We had even created a Tribeca Citizen of the Year award, hosted the event in one of the De Niro's restaurants, and handed out plaques to untrustworthy politicians, including Deborah Glick and the term-limited city council member, hoping they'd help us. Now I was collecting money to pay for lawyers and lobbyists, and bundling campaign contributions to give to a politician who was as likely to betray us for the real estate money as to help us. I told myself it was for a good cause, probably what all those people who take Mike's money tell themselves.

I had been to very few political fundraising events, let alone one in the home of a former Secretary of the Treasury. But I wasn't interested in standing around listening to political speeches. I told Ethan the money would be there, but I wouldn't. He urged me to attend, shake hands with Miller, and bring along four guests. I had to go.

I invited José Torres, a former light-heavyweight boxing champion who lived at Independence Plaza; David Jones, the head of the city's largest social service organization; and two other tenants. Jones wrote a regular column in the *Amsterdam News*, the largest black-owned daily newspaper in New York. Torres wrote an occasional column for New York's largest Spanish-language daily.

Jones, an old family friend, had been following our fight and early on had set up an exploratory meeting with Betsy Gotbaum, the Public Advocate who had succeeded Mark Green. I hoped she would become a bridge to Bloomberg. But she had a public falling out with him over his attempt to change the city charter so as to eliminate her job and to elect city officials through so-called nonpartisan elections—nice work for a Republican in a 5–1 Democratic town. The voters decisively rejected it, something Mike wouldn't give them an opportunity to do on term limits. I abandoned the Gotbaum approach.

As soon as we entered the lobby of Rubin's Park Avenue cooperative, the Spanish-speaking uniformed doormen and building workers crowded around José Torres. They laughed, hugged, and chatted with him in Spanish—what a scene it was. I was surprised. José's next-door neighbor, whose family was from Cuba, had driven us uptown. We leaned against the lobby wall and watched the outpouring of affection.

"I never realized that José was that big," I remarked to my Cuban-born neighbor.

"Neil, José is the Hispanic Muhammad Ali." It was something to keep in mind.

An elevator operator wearing white gloves took us up to the Rubin apartment. Thirty or forty people were milling about, munching on canapés and sipping cocktails. The guests were well-to-do New Yorkers whose politics I might have once found congenial. In any case, they had little interest in affordable housing. Had I been one of the Park Avenue co-op crowd, I suppose I wouldn't have been interested either.

Robert Rubin stayed in the background. This was his wife's fundraiser. It was focused on the arts. Judy Rubin walked to the front of the room, welcomed everyone, and introduced Ethan.

He said a few words about Miller's unyielding support for the arts and introduced him. Miller thanked everyone for being there and told them how passionate he felt about the arts. A few friendly questions, followed by Ethan's thank-you to the Independence Plaza guests, and the formal part was over. We mingled a bit and left.

Judy Rubin sent a nice thank-you note and that was that. We had the Council speaker and a veto-proof majority. We were by no means home free, but I was feeling better about things. I was about to find out just how far the determined little guy would go to get his way.

CHAPTER EIGHT

Mike Unleashed

◄○►

A t 10 a.m. on October 29, the day of the rally and hearing that Miller had scheduled to introduce his bill, Mike held a press conference in City Hall's Blue Room. With housing commissioner Jerilyn Perine standing at his side, he announced a state legislative "initiative" that would extend rent stabilization to all Mitchell-Lama tenants whose developments were being bought out.

Mike was signalling to the public his support for all Mitchell-Lama tenants, tens of thousands of families, knowing that his initiative had no chance of ever becoming a law. He was introducing his version of a Vito Lopez one-house bill! In fact, where Democrats like Lopez may have been indifferent, Mike was worse: He actively opposed rent stabilization for Mitchell-Lama tenants or anyone else for that matter. That's why he was proposing his own bill, one that Albany would have to pass. I actually thought it was beneath him. I was still learning.

The reporters in the room asked Joe Bruno's spokesman to comment. He said the Senate majority leader hadn't had a chance to review the initiative (other than a press release, there was nothing to review), but "we have not been supportive of efforts to expand rent regulation in the city." Exactly.[53]

At the hearing later that afternoon, State Senator Martin Connor testified that the initiative would "have a long wait in Albany. I serve in the state senate, and I can tell you the likelihood of passing legislation opposed by the real estate lobby is nil. The Council legislation is needed and needed now." Connor, the reader will recall, had hired our former city council member to work up an Albany tenant bill for him to introduce. Now he was conceding that no such bill could ever become law. The political context had changed and now he could tell the truth.

Speaking truth to power sometimes takes courage; speaking truth to the powerless requires integrity. Connor was a veteran politician who had mastered the art of presenting his constituents with bullshit in all its arcane forms. Still, veteran politician though he was, Connor wasn't in Mike's league.

Perine testified. She lauded the council's concern over the loss of affordable housing. Regrettably, the administration would have to oppose Miller's bill. She said the council had no authority to enact it. (A legal scholar who held a named chair at the NYU Law School testified that the bill was well within the Council's authority.) The bill wouldn't stop owners from leaving the program anyway, she said.

Perine understood, of course, that our purpose was not to stop the owners—we knew we couldn't—but rather to give tenants some leverage to negotiate reasonable settlements.

She laid it on thick. She had a better idea than Miller's bill: "Let's all work together with the governor and the state legislature to achieve passage of this crucial legislative initiative and protect the viability of this important housing stock."

"If you don't get your proposal passed in Albany, what's plan B?" one council member asked her.

"We'll do everything we can to pass the bill. There is no plan B." Everyone but the *New York Times* reporter understood there was no plan A either. Actually, I didn't know whether the reporter understood or not. I'll introduce him momentarily.

Eventually, Mike sent a bill up to Albany. When it arrived, it joined the rest of the one-house bills buried in the bowels of a legislative committee. For any insider who watched this scenario unfold, Mike's character and his intentions became crystal clear. But for the vast majority of New Yorkers who supported him, if they paid any attention at all, here's what they'd read.

◄○►

The *New York Times* lead was:

> *Making a bid to win over the city's sizable and vocal tenant population, Mayor Michael R. Bloomberg yesterday proposed adding 32,000 units to the number of rent-regulated apartments in New York City.*

Times reporter David Chen ignored the Miller bill—as did Miller who, Chen wrote, "told reporters at the rally that the mayor's proposal was 'a good step in the right direction.'" I should have realized that Miller was about to walk away from his own bill. I didn't.

Compare the *Times* story with the November 18, 2003 editorial published in the local paper, *The Downtown Express*:

> *The prospects of the mayor's bill passing the Republican-controlled state senate are slim, if they are that good. ... The Bloomberg administration and the real estate industry argue that the Council bill is illegal because the city can't pass a law changing the state law. We can't be sure who is right, but we are confident the Independence Plaza tenants stand a better chance defending this proposed city law in court than waiting for Bruno to get an 11th hour conversion and back new rent protections.*

Chen followed up with another story on November 19, 2003. The headline read "Bit by Bit, Government Eases Its Grip on Rents in New York."

"Eases its grip" suggests that the government's grip had been too tight. A more accurate headline might have been something like "Government Stands Aside While

Taxpayer-Financed Developments Are Deregulated and Landlords Reap Windfall Profits." But the headline writer was faithful to Chen's piece. Chen characterized rent stabilization as "a vast rent-regulation system that has guaranteed rent ceilings for tenants at all income levels for decades."

What fair-minded person could favor a regulatory system that protects even the wealthy from rent increases? It's true that some high-income tenants game the system, but large systems always have cheaters at the margins. When a landlord discovers a wealthy celebrity occupying a six-room, rent-regulated apartment on Manhattan's West Side, the story is likely to appear in the *New York Times* or one of the tabloids. The vast majority of tenants in rent-stabilized apartments are poor to moderate-income people. The median income (half higher, half lower) is $38,000.

Chen was reprising Ronald Reagan's Welfare Queen, the mythical woman who walks into the welfare office wearing a mink coat, while her boyfriend waits outside in a Cadillac. This anecdotal outlier is an old political ploy used to delegitimize social programs.

Chen went on to use the familiar *Times* formula: on the one hand, X, and on the other hand, Y.

"Landlords and free-market advocates," he wrote, "are finally seeing an end to a failed social experiment that became an entitlement," one that created "bewildering inequities" and "discouraged construction of new housing ..."

He continued:

> *For tenant advocates and their political patrons, these events signal something frightening: the passing of an era in which government believed that part of its essential mission, along with dispensing welfare checks and Medicaid, was helping to provide shelter, particularly in New York, where the cost of living is steep.*

According to Chen and thus to the *New York Times*, tenants are in league with politicians, they are associated with welfare checks, and they rue the passing of an era. Landlords just want to get rid of entitlements, inequities, and failed social experiments.

It was a long piece, and there was much more of the same. Mike's political razzle, buttressed by the *New York Times* and all that real estate money flowing into politics, would be hard to overcome. Our fight was about to take a new turn.

Miller Folds

Miller decided not to advance the bill he had sponsored. Instead, he offered to mediate between Gluck and the tenants. I had earlier told Ethan that if Miller betrayed us, I would lead a citywide demonstration of tenants who would carry signs, *Speaker with Forked Tongue.* Mike's initiative and the *New York Times* response to it made it an empty threat: If we rejected the offer to mediate, he would announce that he had forced the mayor to act. He'd wait to see what happened in Albany.

Of course, we all knew what would happen. The *New York Times* would report it just that way. Miller would pick up the real estate money, take the political cover that Mike had given him, and we might well lose our homes. We were going to have to negotiate without a bill.

The negotiations dragged on for three months. Gluck and I sat across from one another, flanked by lobbyists and lawyers. He engaged in various maneuvers to run the clock right up to the midnight hour, when he could legally exit the program without giving an inch. His main housing expert, a former HPD lawyer, met privately with Julie Walpert, the assistant commissioner in charge of the city's Mitchell-Lama program. Walpert made unprecedented, legally questionable decisions that tilted the negotiations in Gluck's favor. She then wrote a long letter to Gluck's lawyer (copy to the file), claiming that her decisions were made to help the tenants. We didn't learn about them until after the negotiations ended.

They had begun in December 2003. Late in February 2004, I told Ethan, who had sat through every session, even though he had been named the New York coordinator for Howard Dean's ill-fated presidential run, that I had scheduled a tenant meeting two weeks hence to announce that the negotiations had failed. We would have no choice but to go to court. Ethan persuaded me to postpone the meeting and keep negotiating. I must say here that without him, we wouldn't have been at the negotiating table at all.

Gluck and I went back and forth on the bottom-line issue: How far and how fast did he propose to raise the rents once he left the Mitchell-Lama program? Gluck, after walking out of the meeting once and engaging in some other theatrical ploys, finally agreed that for those tenants not eligible for housing vouchers, the rent would be whatever rent stabilization rates were established by the Rent Guidelines Board plus 1 percent. I was relieved. I would now hold the tenant meeting to announce that we had a deal and ask for a vote of approval.

But after we had agreed in principle on the basic terms, Gluck demanded an additional 10 percent in the tenth year of the agreement. His explanation for the changed position was, "I have an itch." Or as Mike might have put it, *fuck you and have a nice day.*

Nothing in the negotiations had angered me as much. I could walk out, but it was getting close to the June deadline when he could exit the program. Miller would be no help. I couldn't risk making the wrong call. Gluck won the game of chicken. I agreed to the deal, which may have been as good as I could have gotten, disliking him all the more but nonetheless relieved that it was over.[54]

When we announced the deal in that same 800-seat auditorium, tenants gave us a standing ovation. They were as relieved as I was.

We signed the deal in Gluck's lawyer's offices. "I feel like we just signed the Oslo Accords," Gluck said.

"Let's hope this deal has a better outcome," I replied.[55]

Mike Makes History

The deal was reported in the *Times* on March 9.[56] The account was brief. On March 15, 2004, the administration issued the following press release:

MAYOR MICHAEL R. BLOOMBERG ANNOUNCES AGREEMENT BETWEEN OWNERS AND TENANTS OF INDEPENDENCE PLAZA
Agreement on Rents Maintains Affordability for Existing Tenants
Mayor Michael R. Bloomberg today announced an agreement between the owners and tenants of Independence Plaza on a plan to keep rents afford-able at the 1,332-unit Mitchell-Lama development in Lower Manhattan.

"Former HPD Commissioner Jerilyn Perine was instrumental in bringing the two parties together to ultimately reach this agreement, and this resolution will keep rents affordable for tenants, thereby relieving the anxiety that comes with the sale of the development," said Mayor Bloomberg.

Neither Mike nor his administration had anything to do with the settlement, except that they made it more difficult for us to reach one. But *New York Times* readers would never know the truth. Three months later, David Chen wrote:

In March, for instance, the city helped to broker a deal between the tenants and owner of the Independence Plaza housing development in Tribeca to protect tenants from escalating rents once the development leaves the Mitchell-Lama program this year.[57]

That is now the official history. Chen quoted me as having said that tenants "are delighted that this settlement will enable them to continue to live in affordable housing for years to come." I never met or spoke with Chen.

◄○►

After the settlement, I resigned from the tenant association board. Gluck refinanced Independence Plaza for about $425 million. Two-bedroom apartments for new tenants are going for more than $5,000 a month. The families who once lived here are gradually giving way to single professionals who are sharing apartments. I seem to be the only person on the elevator carrying a newspaper rather than a digital device. Yes, it's a *New York Times*. Long ago, I broke the habit of the *New York Post*, but the *Times* is harder to give up.

Gifford Miller received a large amount of money from the real estate lobby but came in fourth in the 2005 Democratic mayoral primary. The Mitchell-Lama bill he sponsored but declined to pass has not been reintroduced by his successor.

In January 2006, Gluck joined the executive committee of the Real Estate Board. According to published reports, he had a net worth of $425.7 million and liquid assets totalling over $92.7 million. In 2006, the Associated Builders and Owners of New York gave him its Developer of the Year award. Gluck went on to acquire some fifteen rent-regulated developments with the same idea: getting them deregulated, driving up the rents, and cashing in. When the financial crisis hit, he had trouble holding on to some of them. He may have lost some anticipated profits, but I doubt he's lost any of his own money.

This excerpt from a collection of essays on the suburbanization of New York describes my neighborhood today:

> *Thanks to gentrification, that home, that vibrant, dynamic, artistic community—the Tribeca of my youth—no longer exists ... more than $800 million worth of Liberty Bonds were issued to development companies to build massive residences ... [it] paid for the creation of luxury condos in order to lure a specific kind of resident.*[58]

Of course, it isn't only Tribeca that has undergone the transformation from local neighborhood to Luxury City. Walk along Madison Avenue, a few blocks from Mike's townhouse, and look at the window displays, the grotesque jewelry, the luxury leather goods, the ball gowns—the glitzy stores guarded by the inevitable uniformed black man. Mike continues to work at transforming a cosmopolitan city that once had some character into a sterile, increasingly unaffordable city for all but the rich and for young people without kids.

As for me, I was glad to be done with organizing tenants, done dealing with meretricious politicians and housing bureaucrats, and, most of all, done with Mike. Jane Jacobs, the famous grassroots activist-writer who fought Robert Moses for decades, once told an interviewer, "I hate the government for making my life absurd." I'm no Jane Jacobs, but I know how she must have felt.

When I decided to write this book, Arlo Chase, one of our more cerebral lawyers who had drafted the city council legislation that Miller agreed to sponsor, urged me to take up the challenge of writing "theory, theory, theory." But as the reader knows by now, I'm not a theorist. I'm a lawyer by training. I came to politics by accident, and by accident backed into the Independence Plaza tenant presidency. In telling Mike's story and that of Independence Plaza, I wanted only to peel back the curtain on the deceptive politics we faced in trying to save our homes.

In my research, I came across a largely forgotten and somewhat hidden history of New York. I tell that story next in Book Two. I hesitated to tell it at any length because it's not for everyone, not even for political junkies. But it's a "follow the money" story and it has to be told. The last thing the insiders want you to do is precisely that—follow the money— so they make it exceedingly difficult. (I still can't quite get my head around inverse floating-rate notes.) But as the money is so central to everything about New York, it's crucial to understand where it came from and where it went: the source and the flow. It wasn't so easy to find out what really happened the last time New York went broke. The insiders didn't want anyone to know where the money went—then or now.

It was not the banks that created the mortgage crisis ... It was, plain and simple, Congress who forced everybody to go and to give mortgages to people who were on the cusp [and who] pushed Fannie and Freddie to make a bunch of loans that were imprudent; they were the ones that pushed the banks to loan to everybody.

—Michael Bloomberg, November 1, 2011

BOOK TWO

Follow the Money

—◄o►—

Those who cannot remember the past are condemned to repeat it.
George Santayana

CHAPTER ONE

Back to the
Future

I don't know whether George Santayana's famous dictum is true, but merely remembering the past isn't enough to avoid repeating it. The question is whether we can stop those who are bent on repeating it. The fairly recent past is easy to remember. Wall Street's financial engineers looted the country in the 1980s, the era of hostile tender offers and leveraged buyouts. They seized control of productive enterprises, loaded them with massive debt, dramatically reduced their taxes, stripped away their assets, cut back on research and development, and fired employees. They did these things in the name of efficiency. They invested little or none of their own money, they took few or no risks, and they enjoyed fabulous profits. In their wake they left devastated communities whose economic life depended on these once-productive companies. And they sharpened dramatically the disparity of wealth and income that we see today. Some of these leveraged buyout operators became great philanthropists; some presidential candidates.

They did it again a few years ago, this time loading up unsophisticated home buyers with unsupportable debt, securitizing the debt, bribing credit rating agencies to tack on triple A ratings, and selling the worthless securities around the world. They are doing it today, and they will do it again tomorrow. The names of the players and the financial instruments they invent are different, but the motives are always the same and have nothing to do with the public or anyone else's interest.

A close-grained look at how they did it to New York City in 1975 and what happened next is instructive. It has much to do with how the city looks and is governed today. Until our fight at Independence Plaza ended and I began working on this book, I hadn't a clue as to the role played by the Mitchell-Lama program in bringing about the city's last great financial crisis.

Every politician we encountered (except for our congressman) told the Mitchell-Lama tenants the same story: The state had made a deal with the landlords that if they took limited profits for a limited period of time (twenty years), they could then exit the program and go to market rents. That deal had to be honored. I accepted the story of limited profits at face value. I discovered that the federal appeals court had rejected the claim of a deal, ruling that when state governments want to enter into a contract they know how to do it. They hadn't done it here. There had been no "deal," certainly not a legal one. The state had simply amended the original Mitchell-Lama legislation and had given landlords the right to exit the program. But forget the legalities, had the landlords in fact limited their profits? Had they taken risks? Invested their capital? These are the rationales for profit-taking in a market-based system. What was the real deal? The money deal.

◄O►

Decades earlier Harold Cohn had hired Jerry Belson, a prominent real estate operator, to help get the Independence Plaza project approved and publicly financed. He
had been there at the creation. Now he headed the Associated Builders and Owners
of New York that had given Gluck its Developer of the Year award. After the settlement, I called him. His secretary put him on the phone.

"You got a good deal from Gluck," was the first thing he said.

"Some tenants don't think so," I replied.

"They're nuts."

"Will you talk to me?"

"I'll give you an hour at eleven on Thursday."

I stepped off the elevator on the sixth floor of a seven-story office building on
Broadway, a few blocks from Independence Plaza. The sign on the entrance read
Jerome Belson Enterprises. I liked that word—*Enterprises*. It conveyed the idea
that here is a man of many parts; but as to what they were, who could say?

A small, sixtyish, energetic-looking woman greeted me.

"What are you seeing Mr. Belson about?"

"I'm thinking about writing a book on real estate and politics."

She looked up at me with a kind of good-humored, puckish suspicion. "If you're
good, I'll let you see Mr. Belson." The motherly gatekeeper had been with him for a
long time, thirty-five years, as it turned out.

There's a lived-in feel to these old-style New York offices: walls that need a
paint job, dim lighting, old brown office furniture, a few phones, a couple of ancient
desktop computers, a fax machine, papers and files strewn about. There was only
the one woman and a middle-aged guy in a suit who seemed to be working for her.
It was just the opposite of those upscale Midtown Manhattan law offices where the
reception areas display inoffensive abstract paintings picked out by interior deco-
rators and the business weeklies are neatly arranged on the coffee tables between
the leather couches. Eventually, your lawyer comes out to lead you into the inner
sanctum, where you start running up the $500-per-hour fees that pay for the paint-
ings and the decorator. Laurence Gluck had plenty of those kinds of lawyers.

Belson is an old-school Brooklyn guy. We're not paying for overhead that we don't
need, is what these offices said to me, the Brooklyn sensibility of my parents' genera-
tion: low overhead, serious business. I liked the feel of it. I didn't expect to like him.

The receptionist led me along a corridor lined with photographs, letters,
wooden plaques, and awards that attested to a busy philanthropic life. We reached
the end of the long corridor; she knocked on a closed door, opened it without waiting for an answer, and announced, "Mr. Belson, this is Mr. Fabricant."

Belson's private lair fit the overall decor. An eccentric, very big, horseshoe-
shaped table dominated the large, windowless room. It looked as though it had

occupied that space for decades, as did its owner. He was sitting in a swivel chair in the opening in the table's U, looking at a computer screen, his back to me. "Have a seat; I'll be right with you."

I sat down across the table and waited. Ordinarily I would have been annoyed that he hadn't even looked up when I walked in, but I had the impression he wasn't doing it for effect. He seemed genuinely absorbed by the information on the screen. I could see rows of numbers. A few seconds later, he turned around, leaned across the desk, and shook my hand.

"Thanks for seeing me," I said. He nodded.

Belson was in his eighties when we met, a burly guy with a round face framed by a white beard, big round glasses, and wisps of long white hair scattered at different angles around his head. In his heyday he had managed as many as 20,000 apartments in the city. He was full of energy, still doing business. At this stage in his life, I hoped he would tell me the true backstory of Independence Plaza.

"We built it as a rental from the beginning," Belson explained. "We had the land, the property-tax abatements, the tax deductions for the limited partners, and the rest of the benefits that went with its being a Mitchell-Lama. We opened in the fall of 1974, but there weren't enough people who would pay $85 a room to move into a neighborhood that was still old industrial buildings and warehouses without a supermarket."

Belson got the City to support a federal mortgage subsidy worth about $3.5 million a year. The 1 percent interest rate brought the rentals down to $62 a room and the apartments filled up quickly.

As part of the deal, Harold Cohn agreed to set aside 20 percent, or 266 apartments, for low-income tenants whose rents were capped at 30 percent of their gross incomes. Independence Plaza would be even more racially and economically integrated.

We had spoken for a few minutes. It was interesting, but he wasn't telling me anything about the politics or how the money flowed, which is what I wanted to know. I mentioned Charles Gargano, who still sat in the middle of the Pataki–D'Amato real estate money machine.

He looked surprised. "I see you've been around."

I wanted him to think so. I thought he might tell me some deeper truths. He did. I learned that the roots of our fight went back to the 1920s.

—◄o►—

Joseph Belsky, Belson's father, had been secretary to the Hebrew Butcher Workers' Union 234. The butcher workers were Jewish immigrants, many of whom lived in what was then a hellhole, and today is the hip, almost unaffordable Lower East Side. Two small rooms in a six-story tenement might have housed as many as twenty-five people. Many workers slept in the back of unheated, foul-smelling butcher shops.

In 1926, Governor Al Smith established the Limited Dividend Housing Companies Law. The law was structured so that the people ended up owning their own homes. Fast-forward to the 1950s and New York's acute postwar housing shortage. By then, Joseph Belsky was a vice president of the Amalgamated Meat Cutters and Butcher Workmen of North America. The union built a limited-dividend cooperative, 288 apartments in three six-story elevator buildings in Brooklyn. Belsky was proud of the accomplishment and had written a small book about it:

The Harry Silver Apartments is owned and operated by the occupants— there will be no profits for outside interest, and any surplus will be passed on to the tenant-owners in the form of lower future maintenance charges. ... My members own their apartments! They are no longer at the mercy of landlords, who would put them out to get more money for their apartments.

The cooperative was financed with a low-interest loan from a friendly bank. The union member put up about $400, which was the only equity in the deal. He could even get a bank loan for it. The workers would own their apartments. If someone moved out, the cooperative bought back the shares, gave the seller his money back, and the apartment went to the next person on the waiting list. Jerry Belson was the union's lawyer and helped put the deal together. "That," he said, "is how I got started in the real-estate business."

The Harry Silver Apartments in Brooklyn was one of eleven cooperatives that unions sponsored under the limited-dividend law, the forerunner to Mitchell-Lama. The cooperative opened in 1953 and soon had a waiting list of more than a thousand people.

Before Gluck got control, we had wanted to transform Independence Plaza into just such a cooperative. Nobody would get rich, people would own their own apartments, and the complex would remain affordable for future generations. A righteous thing all around and I thought it would insulate us from the charge that we, not the landlord, wanted to cash in on the hot real estate market.

Here's Mike at a public forum after our settlement with Gluck:

Remember, the tenants in Mitchell-Lama want to buy their apartments. They're fundamentally not on the side you'd think they are. Some activists are. But the people who live in Mitchell-Lama houses, they would make a fortune on buying their apartments in this day and age when we don't have enough housing.

I asked Belson why, since the taxpayers were putting up the financing, more of the Mitchell-Lama developments weren't built as limited-dividend cooperatives. He agreed that the cooperatives were a good thing, but there was much more money to be made in owning a rental building. (My words, not Belson's.) He talked about tax shelters and fees, but it was hard to follow. I knew about the corruption, but I had always assumed that the "limited profit" Mitchell-Lama program had capped the legal returns at 6 percent. Belson had given me the first clue that there were indeed deeper truths that few know about to this day.

Always Follow the Money

In 1955, three years before Nelson Rockefeller became governor, New York was facing an acute housing shortage. The FHA redlined entire city neighborhoods populated by immigrants and minorities. No FHA insurance meant no mortgages, and no mortgages meant no affordable housing. The city was losing its middle class to the suburbs, where people could buy single-family homes with small down payments, extended FHA mortgage amortization schedules, low interest rates, and tax deductions.

Governor W. Averell Harriman signed into law the Limited Profit Housing Company Act. Under it, the state would finance 90 percent of a housing development's costs for up to fifty years at below-market interest rates. Developers could get property-tax abatements on cheap land in marginal neighborhoods where real estate taxes weren't being collected anyway. In return for the subsidies, they agreed to limited profits. Development costs were reduced and rents were regulated. The law prohibited owners from exiting the program. That was the deal.

The mechanics were simple: The housing agency issued a mortgage-loan commitment, the developer got a construction loan from a commercial lender, and when the project was completed, the state took out the lender and held the long-term mortgage.

Financing for the program came from a $50 million bond issue that the voters had approved in a statewide election. Unions and non-profits flooded the housing agency with applications totalling more than $300 million for the $50 million fund. They built limited-dividend cooperatives—the Harry Silver model.[59]

The Real Estate Board of New York (REBNY) railed against the program, calling it "socialism." Most of the projects would be built in New York City, so it was a simple matter for REBNY to convince upstate and suburban legislators to join it in opposing a second bond issue.

Rockefeller succeeded Harriman and resurrected the program. He borrowed billions of dollars and created what would become one of the most successful affordable housing programs in the nation's history. It came to be known as Mitchell-Lama for its legislative sponsors, McNeil Mitchell, a Republican state senator from Manhattan's East Side, and Alfred Lama, a Democratic assemblyman from Brooklyn.

Rockefeller had $100 million available from a bond issue the voters approved when he was elected. A task force he established recommended that he leverage that money to establish a $300 million fund. Banks and insurance companies would finance an estimated 21,000 units, triple what could otherwise be built by state financing alone. But, like Mike, Rockefeller was thinking billions.

To reduce the lending risk, he established the Limited-Profit Housing Mortgage Corporation, a pooling mechanism that allowed lenders to invest in the Corporation's mortgage-backed securities rather than in individual projects. Still, without a state guarantee, the lenders wanted higher interest rates, which would drive up costs and defeat the program's purposes.[60] The problem, therefore, was how to borrow very large sums at low interest rates without pledging the state's general revenues, a pledge that would require voter approval.

—◄◦►—

John Mitchell, then a New York bond lawyer and later Richard Nixon's attorney general, came up with the idea of the Moral Obligation Bond. Legally, the bondholders could look only to the rents or maintenance payments for their money, not the general treasury, but the bond resolutions provided that if the revenues generated by the project (i.e., rents) were insufficient, the legislature would be "morally obligated" to appropriate the funds necessary to service the debt. That's how the issuance of moral rather than general obligation bonds kept interest rates low and finessed the need for voter approval.

Rockefeller's lawyers faced one more hurdle: Federal law allowed commercial banks to underwrite only general obligation bonds. The lawyers persuaded the US Comptroller of the Currency that for purposes of federal law, the moral obligation bonds were really general obligation bonds, but for purposes of state law, they weren't. Thus the state could issue the bonds without violating state law and the banks could buy and sell them without violating federal law; a dubious proposition, but rich, powerful clients always have lawyers who find a way. Think Alberto Gonzalez, John Yoo, and the torture memos.

By 1975, thirty states had established public authorities that floated billions of dollars in moral obligation debt. It was like printing money. The proceeds from New York's bonds financed the Mitchell-Lama affordable housing program.

◄○►

Politicians, of course, wrap all such programs in the rhetoric of public purpose. More prosaic objectives generally determine their fate: Who pays? How much? Who benefits? Who controls?

John Mitchell's law firm became the housing agency's bond counsel. Kidder, Peabody, a century-old Wall Street firm, sold the bonds. The legal and underwriting fees were based on non-competitive contracts, a bonanza for the lawyers and underwriters. Arthur Levitt, the state comptroller, complained about the non-competitive contracts, but he didn't or couldn't stop them.

Institutional lenders bought the bonds for their own portfolios and also sold them to investors who wanted the tax-exempt income. The Mitchell-Lama limited partners put up modest amounts of equity, sometimes as little as 1 or 2 percent. They took accelerated depreciation and other deductions that sheltered income from other sources. The 6 percent returns hardly mattered. There was very little equity in the deals anyway. But the tax deals earned them an estimated 18 percent annual return. That was just the beginning.

The developers held the general partnership interests and controlled the projects. They sold the tax-shelter deals through syndication brokers and pocketed large up-front profits. They also got Builder and Sponsor Profit and Risk Allowances (BSPRA). These were calculated at 10 percent of the replacement cost of the project, less the appraised value of the land. Independence Plaza was a $70 million project. There was more.

The housing regulators routinely approved non-competitive management contracts, often for large six-figure annual retainers. Developers established separate entities for providing security, maintenance, and other services to their own developments. They collected exorbitant fees and won rent increases based on the inflated costs. As is the case today, government oversight was poor or non-existent.

With so many insiders making so much money, the program thrived. It produced affordable housing for hundreds of thousands of moderate-income New Yorkers. The subway stops, streetlights, public schools, parks, newly paved streets, and other amenities that the government provided to service the developments transformed marginal areas into desirable neighborhoods.

Few noticed that the real estate lobby had pushed through a 1959 amendment to the law that allowed owners to prepay their mortgages and exit the program right after fifteen years (the next year it was amended to twenty) without repaying any portion of the subsidies or tax abatements they had received. All they had to do was refinance their mortgages and exit. For most building, rents would be deregulated.

Those profits were more or less legal, but when a dollar moved toward a Mitchell-Lama development it ran a gauntlet of kickbacks, illegal fee splitting, and corrupt practices. General contractors selected subs without competitive bidding. The subs "loaned" money to the general contractors. The loans weren't meant to be repaid; the subs simply overbilled the jobs. Builders inflated their costs through bogus change orders. Shoddy construction was the rule.

Property tax abatements were based on land appraisals. If the appraisers wanted to keep getting work, they rubber-stamped the appraisals already agreed on between the developer and the housing officials. Developers bought city land at public auction and resold it to themselves at big mark-ups. Builders didn't bother to bid on the jobs unless they had the right political connections.

Far from being socialistic, Mitchell-Lama was vintage democratic capitalism: the coupling of government bureaucrats with real estate developers, liaisons blessed by elected officials who were paid handsomely for the service.

—◄o►—

McNeill Mitchell, a lawyer, chaired the legislative committee that oversaw the program. Alfred Lama, an architect, was the committee's vice-chairman. It was a bipartisan project—both men made a bundle.

Jerry Belson explained to me, "You'd give Al a set of plans that had been approved and used in other developments. You told him just to follow those plans." That was small change compared to Mitchell's profits.

Mitchell organized at least twenty-one Mitchell-Lama projects. Herman Cohen, his law partner, was the executive director of the legislative oversight committee. He, too, organized Mitchell-Lama developments. They did their business right out of the committee's offices. Mitchell said he was saving the taxpayers' money.

When questioned by the State Investigation Commission, he said, "Far from having any conflict of interest, we were performing a public service in filling a void … Where [the money] comes from, I don't know, but we know it doesn't come from any payments made by the state over and above regular allowances." He denied sharing any fees with builders, but acknowledged that the practice existed: "That's just what's happened through the ages. It's a way of life." That much was true.

CHAPTER TWO

New York's
1975 Fiscal Crisis

◄○►

THE 1% SOLUTION

Then, as now, the bankers and real estate barons made fortunes, many politicians profited personally, and almost all had their careers underwritten by those same bankers and real estate barons. To paraphrase George Bernard Shaw, the politicians worked for tips. A different financial scheme—the ironically named *moral obligation bond*—was employed and promoted behind the same high-minded purpose: putting people into homes they could afford. Then, as now, the money ran out, the credit dried up, and New York took a very big hit.

The triggering event occurred in February 1975, when the state's Urban Development Corporation defaulted on the moral obligation bonds it had issued to finance 35,000 units of Mitchell-Lama housing. The agency held about $1 billion in Mitchell-Lama mortgages. About $100 million was already in arrears and uncollectible. The default set off a chain of events, the consequences of which the city is still living with.

Before shutting off the city's credit, the bankers quietly dumped $2.3 billion worth of city debt on their own customers. Think Goldman Sachs. In April 1975, they refused to buy $260 million in New York City Tax Anticipation Notes. By June, the debt was $11 billion, about $5 billion of which was in short-term notes. It was more than a New York City problem.

The combined state and city debt amounted to $36 billion, at the time roughly 20 percent of the capital of the entire US banking system. Many urged the city to declare bankruptcy. Lawyers drew up the court papers. But nobody could predict the consequences of the largest municipal bankruptcy in the nation's history. Would businesses flee and further shrink the tax base? Could services be delivered? What about welfare payments? Would a bankruptcy judge declare that the firemen, cops, sanitation workers, teachers, and other city employees had to be paid ahead of creditors? Bankers might throw themselves out of windows, but they wouldn't riot. As in Greece today, folks who depended on a weekly check might.

Gerald Ford never uttered the words in the infamous *Daily News* headline, "Ford to New York City: Drop Dead," but the message was clear: The federal government isn't paying for New York's profligate ways. Alan Greenspan, chairman of Ford's Council of Economic Advisers and an ardent Ayn Rand enthusiast, was opposed to helping the city. Donald Rumsfeld, Ford's chief of staff, and his deputy, Dick Cheney, agreed.

Governor Hugh Carey understood that if the city went down the state would go down with it. He acknowledged that New York had been irresponsible, but pointed out that it was Ford's vice-president, Nelson Rockefeller, who "authorized every fringe and pension benefit and every unwise borrowing Mr. Ford now attacks so righteously; and presidents who diverted tens of billions of dollars to foreign dictatorships and senseless war, and who plunged our economy into its worst crisis in forty years."[61] Sound familiar?

William Simon, Ford's secretary of the treasury, a former Salomon Brothers bond trader who would go on to establish a leveraged buyout firm, spearheaded the political attack: The crisis, he claimed, was caused by liberal politicians: John Lindsay, Abe Beame (New York's mayor when the crisis hit), and the Democrats more generally had forged a political coalition with municipal unions and the poor. Liberal politicians, unions, and poor people had piled up too much debt.

For the ten years before the crisis, the city's municipal wages rose 10.4 percent annually, compared to 6.9 percent in the nine other largest cities, but New York's cost of living was 15 percent higher. Writing several years after the crisis, Charles Morris, a Lindsay budget official, pointed out, "overall changes in employee compensation appear to be not much different from those found anywhere else." In fact, from 1971 to 1975, labor costs fell as a percentage of the budget, from 56.4 percent to 47.4 percent.[62]

Few mentioned the insider profits recounted above. There were many other factors at work. Lyndon Johnson had been waging the Vietnam War abroad while fighting the War on Poverty at home. To a large extent, keeping the first war going required Johnson to finance the second. Richard Nixon would keep Vietnam going, but he had no intention of financing the Great Society and the Democratic urban political base.

Cuts in federal aid programs and housing subsidies, tax policies that encouraged the flight to the suburbs, OPEC's oil embargo, a deep global recession, rising inflation, and a shrinking city tax base—all combined to leave New York holding an empty financial bag of social programs and a municipal payroll that couldn't be sustained. And yes, successive mayoral administrations beginning with Robert F. Wagner Jr., followed by John Lindsay and finally Abe Beame, had gamed the budget system long before the crisis. That was the partial truth behind the "Profligate New York" narrative promoted in Washington.

Abe Beame, a clubhouse politician–accountant who had campaigned on the slogan "He Knows the Buck," insisted that it was only a temporary cash flow problem. It wasn't. The city had to go into the credit markets on a weekly basis at higher and higher borrowing costs. It was at the mercy of the bankers, not a good place to be.

New York had borrowed about $5 billion to finance moderate-income housing. About $1 billion in short-term debt that had been issued in connection with the Mitchell-Lama program was outstanding. Beame continued to roll over the debt, waiting for interest rates to fall. They kept rising.

He and his predecessors had hidden growing deficits with budget gimmicks and phony municipal accounting. Legally required payments into municipal pension funds were finessed by using outdated actuarial tables, and city revenues were accrued, but expenses were booked only when they were paid. The revenues didn't materialize and the expenses came in higher than projected. The city shifted its fiscal-year payments to close budget gaps in one year, making things worse the following year. In the Beame years, it had borrowed on the basis of imaginary revenues, carrying on its books hundreds of millions of dollars of uncollectible real estate tax debt. About $1 billion of annual operating expenses were hidden in the capital budget.

On September 9, 1975, the state took control of the city's finances through the Emergency Financial Control Board (EFCB), led by investment banker Felix Rohatyn and a small group of banking and insurance executives appointed by Hugh Carey. The EFCB devised a rescue package of massive budget cuts, union pension fund investments in Municipal Assistance Corporation (MAC) long-term bonds, and multiyear wage freezes and firings. Ford and his advisers remained adamant: no help for New York.

Hundreds of banks across the country were holding significant amounts of New York debt. Federal Reserve chairman Arthur Burns began softening his position. Foreign governments warned that the city's bankruptcy threatened the international financial system. They told Ford that the city's bankruptcy would be viewed as the bankruptcy of America. New York was too big to fail. Ford bowed to the pressure and agreed to last-minute federal loans and guarantees.

By mid-1976 the city had laid off more than 50,000 municipal employees, including 20 percent of its teachers and police force. Seniority rules meant that minorities were disproportionately affected. Then, as now, those who caused it and benefited from the crisis shifted the blame and the pain to those who had nothing to do with it.

More than a century of free tuition at City University of New York (CUNY) ended. The subway and bus systems began their long series of fare increases. Maintenance on roads, bridges, streets, parks, and water and sewer systems—virtually all infrastructure projects—was deferred for years. The city closed hospitals and medical clinics, reduced library hours, cut services to the bone. Physically, and politically, New York became a very different city: "Calcutta on the Hudson." Explanations for the causes of the crisis generally served the agendas of those who had caused it. The solutions favored the interests of those who had the power to impose them—the same people.

Roger Starr, a *New York Times* editorial writer, was probably the city's most prominent urban policy voice. He promoted a program of Planned Shrinkage, arguing for transit, sanitation, police, and fire-protection cutbacks in poor neighborhoods.[63] Starr wanted to get rid of poor people:

We should not encourage people to stay where their job possibilities are daily becoming more remote. Stop the Puerto Ricans and rural blacks from living in the city ... reverse the role of the city ... it can no longer be the place of opportunity ... our urban system is based on the theory of taking the peasant and turning him into an industrial worker. Now there are no industrial jobs. Why not keep him a peasant?[64]

Despite all the factors that contributed to the city's parlous fiscal condition, it might have muddled through but for the vast borrowing that it had undertaken through Rockefeller's moral obligation bonds. In a report to Hugh Carey, Felix Rohatyn wrote:

The near bankruptcy of New York City was as much due to improvident capital spending as it was to budget gimmickry. The enormous sums lost on its Mitchell-Lama middle-income housing had to be made up by reduced services and higher taxes; the municipal hospital system could still bring the City down.

A Moreland Act Commission report issued in 1976 echoed Rohatyn's findings:

The introduction of the moral obligation concept by the HFA in 1960 for housing projects, the explosive expansion of the HFA role beyond housing to hospitals, universities and mental institutions in the 1960s, and the extension of the moral obligation concept to UDC in 1968, resulted in a vast accumulation of financial risks for the State of New York.[65]

Through it all, the Mitchell-Lama developments remained fabulously profitable. The partners continued to enjoy the tax shelters, taking depreciation write-offs on the full cost of the developments rather than on their modest equity investments. The accrual method of accounting, which recognizes costs when obligations are incurred rather than when they are paid, allowed the partners to deduct their mortgage obligations from taxable income even when they weren't making their mortgage payments.

Richard Kahan, the New York Urban Development Corporation president, summed it up: "Within a few years there was no reason to maintain a [Mitchell-Lama] project anymore. The return on these projects is unbelievable at this point."

Carey memorably announced that the days of wine and roses were over. He threatened to foreclose on the Mitchell-Lama projects. The investors stood to lose the cash they had put up, but, more importantly, through federal recapture proceedings they risked forfeiting the tax benefits they had already enjoyed. They began paying their mortgages—slowly. And they did just enough maintenance to keep up the buildings—milking them, in other words.

New York Emerges from the Fiscal Crisis: The Koch Years

In January 1978, Ed Koch succeeded Abe Beame.

On April 11, 2011, Mike signed legislation to rename the Queensboro Bridge—or as New Yorkers have known it for a century, the 59th Street Bridge—the Ed Koch Queensboro Bridge. Here's what Mike said at the signing ceremony:

> *When Ed came to City Hall in 1978, New York was reeling from a financial crisis, the streets were dirty, crime was on the rise, and businesses and residents were fleeing for the suburbs. ... Ed Koch launched one of the most remarkable comebacks in history—balancing the books, establishing a sense of order, and before long, people were coming back, new businesses were opening, and New Yorkers began to believe in their in their city again.*

Brooklyn council member Charles Barron said, "Ya'll got to be kidding, a bridge named after Ed Koch. This is not the Ed Koch that black people know." Instead, Barron proposed renaming Riker's Island (New York's notorious dungeon for people serving less than a year and not eligible for state prison) after the former mayor.

These two remembrances, if I can call them that, by two people who see the world very differently mark the city's transition from Calcutta on the Hudson to Hamptons on the Hudson. Much of what New York looks like today, how it was governed before Mike, and how it may be governed after him are rooted in the Koch mayoralty. Here is a brief survey of that period, not so much from Barron's viewpoint, although I'm in agreement with it, but from the interplay of real estate and politics, the indispensable key to understanding how the city works.

Media guru David Garth crafted Koch's campaign slogan, "After eight years of charisma (John Lindsay) and four years of the clubhouse (Abe Beame), why not try competence?" Years later, Mike, also a Garth client, would reprise the non-politician, competent manager theme.

One day during the financial crisis, I can't recall exactly when, a woman passed me by on the street She had three young kids with her, the oldest a boy, maybe thirteen. He and his mother were carrying beat-up old suitcases. Everything they owned. The two little girls were trailing along behind them. They all looked so weary. The boy was lugging the heaviest suitcase. He was trying to look tough. I knew they were heading for some kind of SRO (single-room occupancy) or shelter where he, the man of the family, would have to deal with who knows what kind of evil. As memory and metaphor, that scene remains vividly in my mind; so much of what happened afterward right up to the present keeps reinforcing it.

The city's fiscal condition gradually improved. But times were still tough and many bought into the "Limousine Liberal" narrative that the Republicans and some Democrats, notably Ed Koch, were spinning in those days. (That tag was stuck on John Lindsay by Mario Procaccino, a conservative Democratic. It proved an enduring legacy of the culture wars.) First as a candidate and then as mayor, Koch played on the fears and racial resentments of middle- and working-class whites, becoming a medium of sorts through which the basest instincts were given civic respectability. He flogged the weakened municipal unions, lambasted the "poverty pimps," and insulted black people, albeit in coded terms. When called on it, he issued outraged denials.[66] He did all that in front of the curtain; from behind it, he struck the deals that financed his career and for better or worse helped shape the city's future.

Politics was being rapidly transformed from a labor- to a capital-intensive, television-driven business. Garth's television campaigns were expensive. Koch needed far more real estate money than the mayoral candidates who had preceded him. A Grand Bargain was struck. The elements of that bargain were plain to see in the politics of the day and the results are still visible today.

The bachelor congressman needed a campaign organization outside of his Greenwich Village base. For that, he needed the support of the regular Democratic political clubs controlled by the county leaders—old school political bosses, all of whom had ties to the real estate lobby. The county leaders would provide the field operations and the all-important links to the ethnic outer borough voters that enabled candidate Koch to shed his Greenwich Village image and construct a very different public persona—in point of fact a more authentic one.

For their part, the county leaders needed access to public payrolls to reward their clubhouse loyalists and they needed key municipal appointments to work their business deals, many of them involving real estate. As mayor, Koch could give everyone what s/he needed. In a nutshell, these were the terms of trade between the mayor and the insiders. Tenants had nothing to offer.

In the run-up to the mayoral campaign, Koch came to Meade Esposito's mother's basement for the ritual dinner: meatballs with Meade and a deal.[67] Esposito was the Brooklyn Democratic county leader. He also owned Grand Brokerage Insurance. Some of the city's largest developers were his clients. Stanley Steingut, the Assembly speaker, also from Brooklyn, was his partner.

Only the dinner companions could say what was discussed beyond the meatballs. Except for Koch, they are all dead. One of them was Fred DeMatteis, a large Mitchell-Lama landlord and a Grand Brokerage client who died in the middle of one of the nastiest Mitchell-Lama battles of the 1990s, a precursor to our own struggle with Laurence Gluck. Another was Bobby Wagner, son of the former mayor.

Esposito later bragged to *Village Voice* reporter Jack Newfield, "I get whatever I fucking want from [Koch]." And he did, and so did the other bosses.

Koch appointed Bobby Wagner to chair the City Planning Commission. Wagner by all accounts was an honest man, but he understood what was expected of him. As City Planning chair, among other things, he could authorize a developer to add as much as twenty percent to a development's marketable space. Between 1980 and 1987, developers received 340,000 sq. ft. of bonus space worth $108 million in return for $5 million worth of public amenities.[68]

Developers, architects, lobbyists, real estate lawyers, the people who earn their livings in the subterranean world of real estate and politics, New York's hometown businesses, cultivate good relationships with the New York City Board of Standards and Appeals (BSA). Few New Yorkers know of its existence. Everyone involved with real estate does. The BSA can raise or lower a developer's costs by the way it handles zoning rules and construction practices.

Ed Koch gave control of the BSA to the Bronx, Queens, and Brooklyn county leaders. (Following the corruption conviction of the all-powerful Carmine DeSapio, Manhattan's Tammany Hall had lost much of its political clout.)

Eventually, all three bosses were caught up in political scandals and went to prison or died before they could be put there. The Queens leader, Donald Manes, was caught in the infamous Parking Violations Bureau scandal. Together with the Bronx boss, Stanley Friedman, he controlled a company called Citisource, which had neither assets nor employees, but it did have a crude drawing of a hand-held computer. Koch gave the company a $22 million contract to build hand-held computers for parking meters. It was not shown (or claimed) that Koch pocketed any money, so by New York City standards, many considered him to be an honest politician. Friedman went to jail and Manes committed suicide by plunging a steak knife into his chest. Ed Koch was shocked... shocked.

Peter Solomon, Koch's deputy mayor, an investment banker, was the finance chair for his 1981 re-election campaign. He also chaired the Industrial and Commercial Incentives Board that granted property tax abatements to developers. City Council President Carole Bellamy, who went on to head UNICEF, went public:

I find what is being done outrageous and immoral. ... City Hall is for sale to developers who make large campaign contributions.

Bellamy released a report that identified 22 major developers that had given Koch $388,650. They had received $444 million in tax abatements. The Mayor "talks tenants and acts landlord," Bellamy complained. "For real estate developers and landlords, Ed Koch is the best investment in town."[69]

Koch's famous birthday parties brought to mind the marriage scene from *The Godfather* where the guests brought the money in envelopes and were honored to do so. Heavy jowled or lean and hungry, the bow-tied, tuxedo-wearing landlords and developers came out in force. One birthday celebration raised an estimated $1 million. If the *New York Times* questioned its propriety, I can't recall it.

That event was held at Donald Trump's Grand Hyatt hotel, a fitting venue. Stanley Friedman, who had been Abe Beame's deputy, had arranged for Donald Trump to receive the city's first tax abatement for a commercial property. The abatement was worth $160 million over 42 years. Trump's financing for this, his first major real estate deal, was contingent on it. But the city had no legal authority to grant it. So the Urban Development Corporation took title for $1 and leased it back to Trump for 99 years for a modest rental. Trump paid the city $200,000 a year in lieu of taxes. Robert Tisch, another mega developer, characterized the payment as the "equivalent to the tax bill for a motel on Eighth Avenue."[70] And there you have the rise of Donald Trump. Who's to say New York City—the world— isn't a better place for all those Trump Towers that grace urban landscapes everywhere? The payments in lieu of taxes, or PILOTS, have been used extensively by other mayors, including especially Michael Bloomberg, to lock in place lower taxes for developers for years beyond the term of the mayor who awards them.

Friedman also arranged for a special permit so that Trump could build a restaurant in the hotel jutting out above 42nd Street. You can walk by and still see it today. Friedman then left his government post to join the law firm of the notorious lawyer-fixer, Roy Cohn. Trump was a major client of the firm.

State Senator Franz Leichter of Manhattan, a perennial hair shirt for Koch, released a study revealing that the 25 largest contributors to Koch's campaigns were a dozen major developers and a group of underwriters of the city's bonds. By far the biggest contributor was the Trump Management Corporation. "They are making these contributions because they want favorable action. The line between a bribe and a contribution is almost invisible," Leichter charged. "The perception is that this is an administration for sale."

Koch was livid. "There is a line between libel and hyperbole and in his case it is almost invisible. I don't think there is anything immoral about that at all. From me they get nothing."[71]

Leichter kept hammering away. Koch was indignant. The criticism was a "cheap shot." "Why doesn't Franz Leichter denounce his (Albany) colleagues—that takes guts you know."[72]

Koch, of course, was right about Albany then, as he would be today. But the notion that the developers got nothing for their money was ridiculous. In a nostalgic piece about the New York that once was, Russell Baker, the *New York Times* columnist, said this about the political arrangements between New York's real estate operators and its mayor:

> *Has anybody noticed that New York City is getting darker and darker? If somebody doesn't stop those wonderful people who keep the local builders reaching for the stars, the city will soon be known as the land of the midnight noon ... between the monster buildings embodying the bestial instincts of money-crazed real estate speculators and the architects they corrupted, there was ample space where sunlight fell. ...*
>
> *The old open patches of sunlight are now going dark. Everywhere, monsters are being hurled up toward what we once thought of as Heaven but now regard as the eyrie of tax swindlers, finaglers and similar people too tasteless to be embarrassed about spoiling Heaven.*
>
> *This darkening of the city is commonly attributed to Mayor Koch's encouragement of the real estate and construction boom. Combined with the Wall Street orgies of Reagan days, it turned Manhattan into the home office of grotesque excess and now threatens to put us in the pits.*
>
> *It's dark down here, Ed. Getting dark all over. Ed, your campaign posters should hail you as* The Prince of Darkness. [73]

Mitchell-Lama and moral obligation financing was finished. But Harold Cohn and his partners had squeezed in just under the wire in 1974 with Independence Plaza. Then in the late 1990s when the tax advantages ran out, the real estate market soared, and the statutory obligation to remain in the program expired, it was time for the landlords and developers to make another bundle. And that's what brought me into Mike's World. Let's return now to that magical place.

BOOK THREE

Wall Street's Mayor

—◄o►—

It may be true that you can't fool all the people all the time but you can fool enough of them to run a large country.
Will Durant

CHAPTER ONE

Mike, the
Affordable Housing Mayor

◄o►

In December 2002, Mike announced his New Housing Marketplace Plan. It called for a $3.4 billion commitment to preserve and create 68,000 units of affordable housing by 2008. Later, he expanded it to $7.5 billion and 165,000 units by 2014.[74]

The Biggest and Best the World Has Ever Known!!! There were four-color brochures, photographs of smiling black people, working-class ethnic types, graphs, and charts—the works. Innovative … ground-breaking … pioneering… there weren't enough superlatives to describe it.

Mike then presided over the greatest loss of affordable housing the city has known since the wholesale abandonment in the 1970s. Almost from the beginning of his reign, New Yorkers were ducking under construction ladders, walking through makeshift sidewalk tunnels and beneath scaffolding, and occasionally being killed by the toppling giant cranes. The developers were building luxury condominiums. Mindful of the potential political fallout, Mike distanced himself from the elimination of the city's most important affordable housing stock—rent-stabilized apartments. Each year, the city Rent Guidelines Board establishes the legally permissible rent increases on the city's million-plus rent-stabilized apartments, home to more working New Yorkers than any other type of housing. The median income of people living in those apartments is under $40,000 a year. Mike had a new marketplace housing plan for them too.

Marvin Markus, a Goldman Sachs investment banker, had chaired the RGB from 1979 to 1984. Back then, tenants had nicknamed him "Marvin Markup," as year after year he slammed them with extraordinarily high rent increases.

During Mike's first two terms, Markus, one of Mike's first appointments, ratcheted up rents well beyond the rate of inflation and beyond the ability of hard-pressed tenants to pay. During that same period, the city lost more than 200,000 apartments that rented for less than $1,000 a month. A recent state Assembly study concluded that overall, the city lost 569,700 units of affordable housing between 2000 and 2007 due to destabilization and rent increases. The losses for the remaining years of Mike's mayoralty are likely as bad or worse.

Vacancy decontrol pushed through by the Albany Republicans who Mike financed, and the lack of oversight of landlords who illegally deregulate units by phony repair bills and other techniques, dwarf the amount of new affordable housing units built under the New Housing Marketplace Plan, which itself is something of a shell game. For some projects Mike redefined "affordable" to include apartments that rent for more than $2,500 a month and for households that earn as much as $130,000 a year.

Markus seemed to relish the annual tenant bloodletting. But there was no doubt that he was carrying out Mike's intentions: When one RGB "public" member voted for a rent freeze proposed by the RGB's tenant members, Mike removed him from the board.

Here's Mike: "We are setting the stage for the largest investment in permanently affordable housing for our police officers, nurses, teachers, and public employees and other middle-income New Yorkers. We can secure our future as a city of opportunity, where all New Yorkers can afford to live and pursue their dreams."

Setting the stage for our future? NYU's Furman Center, a real estate–oriented research institute, issued a report that concluded more than a quarter of the city's 171,500 government-subsidized affordable apartments can begin charging market rents by the end of 2015.

Mike claims that his massive rezoning of the city has made room for more affordable housing. But *independent* housing experts point out that increased land values resulting from the rezoning enable developers to build luxury housing that leads to more gentrification for surrounding neighborhoods and more luxury development. For most real estate operators affordable housing is the cover story. Having Mike in City Hall has been a giddy experience.[75]

The very idea that families who have lived in their homes for decades, whose children attend the local schools, whose friends, neighbors, local shopkeepers, and everything that constitutes a community are not regarded by this mayor as stakeholders and are forced out or live in fear of losing their homes so as to maximize the profits of a handful of real estate operators and their bankers is cruel; that it is so often done with taxpayer subsidies behind a mask of tenant and neighborhood-friendly pronouncements is perverse and corrupt.

What follows are a few stories that illustrate Mike's sales approach.

ATLANTIC YARDS

In 2003 Bruce Ratner, real estate developer, former consumer affairs commissioner under Ed Koch, and Friend of Mike, announced his planned $2.5 billion development called "Atlantic Yards."[76] The site was to be twenty-one acres (one acre was added later) in the heart of Brooklyn with fifteen (now sixteen) towers, a sports arena for the New Jersey Nets basketball team to be designed by Frank Gehry, 2.1 million square feet of commercial space, and something north of 4,500 rental units. Ratner was selling his Atlantic Yards project, the largest development project in Brooklyn's history, as a job-creating, affordable-housing engine, a project that would revitalize downtown Brooklyn. The project and the pitch reminded me of a similar Brooklyn real estate story I had witnessed years earlier.

It was 1973 and I was running a research institute based at Baruch College. With its 17,000 students and the city's only public business school, the college has a good reputation as a place where low- and moderate-income students can get credible business and accounting degrees. One day, Baruch President Clyde Wingfield told me that state officials were pushing to relocate the college from Manhattan to a rundown area in downtown Brooklyn. They said the move would create jobs and revitalize the area. As the proposed new site was just over the bridge to Manhattan, they claimed the move wouldn't damage the school. Wingfield thought the idea was so ridiculous and costly that it would just fade away. I knew it wouldn't. I asked some friends in Albany what was going on.

They told me "this is personal," meaning that some important politicians—I didn't ask who they were—were going to make some serious money. They owned real estate in downtown Brooklyn and were in on the deal. They would use various quasi-public and non-profit entities, invoke the state's power of eminent domain to get rid of whatever businesses and residences stood in the way, and get the usual tax abatements, tax-exempt financing, direct subsidies, zoning variances, and so forth. It would be useful to have Baruch in the mix. They could build a new campus. The new construction financed by tax-exempt bonds, subsidies, tax credits, and other benefits would enlist the support of bankers and the construction unions. There would be insurance brokerage, architectural, and engineering contracts. Prominent legislators and party men owned interests in these traditional political sidelines. It would all be done in the name of "revitalization," "job creation," "educational enrichment," and whatnot. Downtown Brooklyn needed improving, but nobody who lived there, and certainly not students, were the intended beneficiaries. It wasn't about them.

Clyde was from Texas, not a reticent political environment. But New York politics is different. Albany is especially hard to understand unless you've been there. The Brooklyn political crowd has always had great leverage in Albany. It was going to be a problem, I told him, more or less in those words. Capital spending was a winning formula for the insiders; getting faculty lines wasn't. They'd come out of the expense budget, would be recurring items, and would only advance Baruch's educational mission.

He was upset and "determined to get to the bottom of it." He made an appointment to see the Brooklyn borough president, a Democratic Party regular tied to the Esposito-Steingut Brooklyn Democratic organization.[77] He returned from his meeting; I could see he was shaken.

"Neil, I made my presentation to the borough president," he reported. "I don't think I could have been any clearer. I reviewed the costs, the disruption, and so on. He just sat there and let me talk. When I finished, do you know what he said to me?"

"Well, I imagine it wasn't pleasant."

"He said, 'That's all well and good, Professor Wingfield, but I'll piss in your ear.'"

I laughed. "Welcome to New York politics, Clyde," where the gap between public purposes and pissing in your ear can be very large indeed. Were it not for the 1975 fiscal crisis, Baruch College would likely be in Brooklyn today.

◄○►

Bruce Ratner eventually developed downtown Brooklyn in the 1990s. MetroTech, a 16-acre, 5.7 million-square-foot office complex, is the city's third largest business district. Ratner said there would be at least 10,000 jobs created. Nobody knows how many jobs were created, what kinds of jobs, or who holds them. But it's a fraction of that number and most are low-paying. Ratner is a real estate developer who saw an urban valley from which he'd make another fortune. He doesn't care about jobs. Pissing in the public's ear is what he does for a living. As always, Mike was in the thick of it. He echoed Ratner's claim:

This project will create tens of thousands of construction and permanent jobs. At this time we really do need these in New York City. They're going to generate tax revenue so we can pay our cops, fire fighters, and teachers, and keep the growth of this city going on.

Here's how things played out.

Eminent Domain

To move ahead with his plan, Ratner had to force out at least 400 families and scores of small businesses that occupied the property he wanted. The state could do that through the power of eminent domain—the taking of private property for public purposes. He needed a finding by the Empire State Development Corporation (ESDC) that the area was "blighted." Ratner marked out the property he wanted, and the ESDC, whose chairman was Charlie Gargano, ruled that the area was blighted.

One appeals court judge commented that the agency was "being used as a tool of the developer to displace and destroy neighborhoods that are 'underutilized.'" The court said it had limited powers of review, and upheld the agency finding.

Cheap Land and Public Cash

The proposed area included 8.5 acres owned by the Metropolitan Transportation Authority (MTA), whose chairman was Peter Kalikow. Like Gargano, he was a top D'Amato–Pataki fundraiser. He was also a real estate developer, and for a brief period the owner of the *New York Post*. I had met Kalikow years earlier in his offices in the Kalikow Building. It was a teaching moment.

Kalikow escorted me across a vast expanse of carpeting, past rows of secretaries clacking away at typewriters, and over to a large set of windows high above Park Avenue. I looked down and saw a typical Manhattan street scene: people crossing, cars and buses, a few stores, and so on. What he saw was a neighborhood a little farther downtown where the buildings were only a few stories high surrounded by much taller buildings. He pointed to it and said, "See that; that's an urban valley." I had never heard the term. We were looking out the same window, but he was seeing zoning variances, public subsidies, rentable square feet, floor area ratios, and so forth—a valley ripe for development.

Peter Kalikow and Bruce Ratner live in Mike's World. The people and small businesses inside the Atlantic Yards site didn't have a prayer.

The MTA negotiated exclusively with Ratner. The agency gave him the property for less than half the appraised value of $214.5 million. The project and the terms of the deal would only get better in the next few years.

In Albany in 2006, the Public Authorities Control Board (PACB), composed of George Pataki, Sheldon Silver, and Joseph Bruno, literally the three men in a room, approved the project. George Pataki proclaimed, "now we can build critically needed housing including affordable housing, new community facilities, grand open spaces and increase economic development all across Brooklyn."

Here are just a few of the salient facts:

- 2009—Ratner sells $511 million in triple tax-exempt bonds at 6.48 percent interest. The sports-arena bonds are backed by payments in lieu of taxes (PILOTs), which, it is claimed, means they won't violate the 1986 federal prohibitions on issuing tax-exempt bonds for sports teams, restrictions that were imposed by the Reagan administration to stop sports arena developers from gouging the taxpayers more than they already do. Mike's lobbyists persuade the Bush Treasury Department to approve the deal.

- 2009—the MTA renegotiates its deal with Ratner. He is required to pay only $20 million up front. The $80 million balance will be paid over 22 years at a low interest rate.
- 2010—the MTA votes to increase subway, bus, and commuter fares for the third time in three years.
- 2010—the *Wall Street Journal* and the *Atlantic Yards Report* reveals that Ratner is trying to raise $250 million for the project from Chinese lenders utilizing the federal EB-5 program. In return for $500,000, each lender would get green cards for all family members.
- 2010—A federal corruption and bribery indictment is brought against political officials in Yonkers. Forest City Ratner is the unindicted, unnamed "Developer No. 2."
- 2011—Forest City Ratner lobbyist Richard Lipsky and state Senator Carl Kruger are indicted on federal corruption and bribery charges. Bruce Bender, a Ratner senior VP and lobbyist, is overheard on a wiretap of Kruger's phones. He wants public funding for two projects, one of which was rebuilding a bridge that had been demolished for the Atlantic Yards project. Kruger says he can only get money for one project. Bender replies that he "doesn't mind fucking the bridge."

Ratner's sports arena will be called Barclays Center. The British bank agreed to pay Ratner $400 million for the name; a price that is later revised downward and is now said to be worth about $200 million. Along with Goldman Sachs, Barclays Capital is the underwriter for the tax-exempt bond sale. The arena will generate revenues from luxury seating, concession sales, licensing deals, sponsorships, naming rights, and other moneymaking opportunities.

Answering the complaint that Ratner was using hundreds of millions of dollars in public subsidies to generate excessive private profits, Assembly Speaker Sheldon Silver says:

> *Our role is not to measure the profits that the private investors will make. Our role is to make sure that state liability on the project will be limited to what they say it will be. And we were satisfied about that, plain and simple.*

Ratner's profits are estimated to be about $1 billion, about as much as the public subsidies he eventually received. One of Albany's heavy campaign contributors, Ratner asks,

"Why should people get to see [Atlantic Yards] plans? This isn't a public project."[78] In a sense, he was right. It wasn't a public project. It was only made to look like one.

Ginned-Up Public Support

The officials who provided the government approvals and public financing were given political cover by "grassroots" support. In January 2004, a state assemblyman announced the creation of a non-profit organization called Brooklyn United for Innovative Local Development (BUILD). A couple of months later, BUILD announced its support for Atlantic Yards. It claimed to represent the community, and began negotiating a so-called Community Benefits Agreement (CBA) with Ratner. In June 2004, BUILD and seven other groups signed the CBA with Ratner. In December 2005, BUILD filed an IRS form listing Ratner as an expected $5 million contributor. Only two of the eight "community" groups that signed off on the deal in 2005 existed before the Atlantic Yards project.

Mike attended the signing ceremony. When reporters questioned the enforceability of Ratner's commitments—they weren't enforceable—Mike stepped in.

Borough President Marty Markowitz, an energetic Brooklyn politician, has perfected the racket of insinuating himself between developers who want to build in Brooklyn and the communities adversely affected by their plans. He "represents" Brooklyn. Typically, he first questions the project: The people of Brooklyn deserve … Brooklyn's future is at stake. That puts him in the game. Markowitz said the Atlantic Yards CBA is "so comprehensive and far-reaching that it puts Brooklyn in a class by itself, at the forefront of the corporate responsibility movement."

Markowitz controls a number of foundations. Reportedly, he has collected some $20 million or more for these entities. Ratner contributed at least $1.7 million and found himself alongside Markowitz, leading the corporate responsibility movement.

A somewhat more socialized but no less odious successor to the borough president who offered to piss in the Baruch president's ear, Markowitz has been fined twice by the Conflicts of Interest Board. The fines are just the cost of doing business—the Goldman Sachs model. Markowitz is Mike's kind of guy.

◄o►

In 2005 Ratner launched something that looked like a tabloid newspaper. He called it *The Brooklyn Standard* and distributed it in Brooklyn alongside real newspapers. It had op-ed pages and even a Letters to the Editor section, including a letter from Markowitz and another from Mike.

One article described Ratner's talk to schoolchildren. He was "relaxed, smiling seated on a child's chair, in his customary humble, winsome manner."

Rev. Herbert Daughtry, pastor of a nearby church, was its author. Taking a page from Mike's playbook, Ratner had signed up for the Rent-a-Reverend program. He put up $50,000 to start Daughtry's non-profit Downtown Brooklyn Neighborhood Association. He promised to give Daughtry control of some seats in the new Nets arena and help with financing a community center and a health center.[79]

Late in 2005, Ratner announced that the project would cost $3.5 billion. (It's now estimated at $4.9 billion.) There would be two-thirds less office space, and there would be more housing.

Of the 6,430 housing units, 1,930 would be luxury condominiums. Frank Gehry is long gone, his $1 billion glass-walled arena replaced by a less ambitious design, at least $200 million cheaper. There will be 100 suites whose average annual lease will be $267,000. Another 15 suites known as "The Vault at Barclays Center" will be for the really high rollers. They'll go for $45,833 a month for minimum three-year leases. Armand de Brignac champagne at $300 a bottle: No luxury will be spared. Brett Yormark, the CEO of Barclays Center and the Nets, told a *Wall Street Journal* reporter, "It enables us to appeal to a different demographic." 2,000 seats in the 20,000 seat arena will be reserved for the hoi polloi at $15 a ticket.

The affordable housing will never be built—or if it is, millions more in taxpayer subsidies will be gotten from some future politicians. The promised public park on the arena's roof is now to be private space.

The Job Creators

Construction unions bought into the Job Creator razzle and supported the project. But after the approvals were had and the court fights were over, Ratner announced plans to prefabricate the housing. A carpenter at a construction site earns $85 an hour in wages and benefits. In the factory, it's $35 an hour. As of February 2011, there were maybe 150 people working at the project site, 19 of them locals. Not only would the prefabricated housing save Ratner millions, it would ensure that if any affordable housing is built, it will consist of studios and one-bedrooms, a transient population. People move and rents increase. Mike and Friends are Job Creators in the Roger Starr tradition.

Bruce Ratner is one of the many developers who contribute to the Mayor's Fund to Advance New York City.[80] When Susan Lerner of Common Cause suggested that large donations from real estate developers for public projects, such as Ratner's donation of $1 million to restore a Coney Island carousel, were blurring the lines between public and private, and between profits and charity, Ratner's press agent, in a fit of faux resentment, replied: "Bruce and Forest City Ratner have indeed supported the rehabilitation of that amusement, and they are guilty of thinking it will be much loved again by kids and their families." How churlish can that woman be, objecting to a new carousel?[81]

City council member Letitia James, the project's leading political opponent, summed it up:

> *He who has money has power, influence, and ultimately politicians. The proposed Atlantic Yards Project is not about jobs or housing, but about bailing out a developer with friends in high places.*

Ratner sold an 80 percent interest in the Nets and a 45 percent interest in the arena to Russia's third wealthiest man, Mikhail Prokhorov, who is said to be a very big basketball fan. The New York City Independent Budget Office concluded that the arena would be a net loss for the city.

STUYVESANT TOWN

Stuyvesant Town–Peter Cooper Village, an 80-acre, middle-class development on Manhattan's East Side, is home to some 25,000 people.

Built by MetLife after World War II, the giant affordable-housing complex was created in the midst of the severe postwar affordable-housing shortage. The city gave MetLife lucrative tax breaks and helped it acquire the land in exchange for an agreement to limit its profit to 6 percent for 25 years and maintain below-market rents. It opened for business in 1947 with more than 100,000 applications. Nearly all the original tenants were young families. After many years of lawsuits and political pressure, MetLife allowed black people to rent some of the apartments.

MetLife decided to sell the complex. About 8,000 of the 11,200 apartments were rent regulated. The bidding began in 2006. The people who lived there pulled together the financing for a $4.5 billion bid, one aspect of which was to keep 20 percent of the total number of apartments as rent-regulated rentals. Another 20 percent would be sold to existing tenants at below-market rates.

Tishman Speyer led an investment group that put in a $5.4 billion bid. It was the biggest residential real estate deal in New York history. Like Bruce Ratner, Jerry and Rob Speyer, father and son, are Friends of Mike. The young Rob chairs the board of the Mayor's Fund to Advance New York City. Jerry is also a board member. He's chaired the Real Estate Board of New York as well as the Federal Reserve Bank of New York. Tishman Speyer is a global real estate empire. New York City is home.

Rob was being groomed to take over the empire. As with New York politics, real estate tends to be a dynastic business. Stuyvesant Town was to be Rob's breakout deal. Jerry said his son had "great vision, wonderful people skills, and loves what he does." What Rob planned to do, of course, was make misery for the 25,000 people whose homes he was about to take over. And the people who lived there knew it.

Tishman Speyer's partner in the deal was BlackRock, a giant global financial firm.

Each partner put up $125 million in equity. Banks and pension funds put in most of the money. (Regrettably, pension funds, who helped fuel the leveraged buyout craze in the 1980s, have a long history of investing in deals that seek large returns and hurt workers.) Merrill Lynch put up $500 million, the second largest piece of financing. It also bought a 49.8 percent interest in BlackRock, a deal that closed shortly before Tishman-Speyer won the bidding war.

About two-thirds of the apartments rented for one-third to one-half of market-rate rentals. The Speyers assured the frightened tenants that they had no conflict with them. They would make their profits by managing the complex "more efficiently." Rob said, "There'll be no radical changes." When tenants asked for details, he said, "It'd be premature to get into the specifics. We are looking for ways to improve the quality of life."

The old crayons and coloring book approach: "You're going to love the changes Mr. Gluck is going to make." "How honored we are," Rob told the Stuyvesant tenants, "to become part of your outstanding community. We look forward to providing you an extraordinary level of service and attentiveness that will be the source of pride and satisfaction for the entire community."

The actual business plan called for deregulating the apartments as quickly as possible and raising the rents dramatically. Housing advocates and most politicians urged Mike to intervene. If there is an iconic middle-class housing complex in New York, Stuyvesant Town is it. How could the Affordable Housing Mayor step aside while the city lost that much affordable housing, never mind the current residents who would lose their homes?

Even the president of the city's Housing Development Corporation weighed in, offering to "use its reserves to make a loan to a buyer that would enable them, in turn, to offer the apartments to current residents at prices they could afford." She added:

MetLife built these properties with help from the city. Do they have any [legal] obligation to do something like this? I think the answer is no. But as long as they can still make a good return on it, why would they not want to do it?

She soon found out why not.

Dan Doctoroff claimed it would be more cost-effective to use city subsidies to build new apartments than to preserve Stuyvesant Town as affordable housing! I'm sure the clever Doctoroff had the numbers to prove it. With Mike and the Boys, we are never far removed from Mark Twain's observation about lies, damn lies, and statistics.

Mike said:

MetLife owns it, and they have a right to sell it. When you have a lot of people wanting to live there, prices go up. You always feel sorry for those who can't afford it, but those who can afford it say "Well, what about me?"

It wasn't about driving up the rents and driving out all those teachers, firefighters, cops, and nurses; it was about being fair to the people who want to move in and could afford it. What about them?[82]

That didn't resonate as well as Mike thought it would. He called a press conference at Stuyvesant Town and assured the assembled tenants: "Jerry Speyer is a great landlord and I think the tenants will be well protected."

Tishman Speyer took control of the property and moved quickly to empty about 1,500 apartments with bogus eviction claims, the ageless landlord tactic of throwing stuff against the wall to see what sticks. They tried to get at least 25 percent of the complex to market rates immediately.

Then it was discovered that MetLife had enjoyed some $23 million in tax breaks to make improvements at Stuyvesant Town. The state's highest court ruled that taking that money meant the complex should never have been deregulated. When the 2008 financial crisis hit, the real estate market tanked, and Stuyvesant Town's value plummeted to less than $2 billion; Tishman Speyer let it go into default. After they walked away, Mike's housing commissioner, Rafael Cestero, said the city's "overriding concern" is that Stuyvesant Town remains affordable for "generations to come."[83]

Years earlier, Mike had agreed with the Conflicts of Interest Board to recuse himself from issues that involved Merrill Lynch, which still held a 20 percent stake in Bloomberg LP.

Wayne Barrett, the city's best investigative reporter on its politics and government, has been dredging the ethical swamp for years. He noted Merrill Lynch's holdings in BlackRock and in Bloomberg LP. Together with its $500 million direct investment in the complex and its 49.8 percent stake in BlackRock, it was the largest investor in the Stuyvesant deal. What was Bloomberg doing endorsing the bid of the largest shareholder in his company against the tenants who lived in the city's largest affordable housing complex?[84]

Barrett submitted written questions regarding the ethical issues raised by Mike's involvement to Stu Loeser, the Mayor's spokesman, who refused to comment or make the city's lawyers available for questioning.

Campaigning for re-election in 2009, Mike's publicists reminded New Yorkers that Mike had initiated "the largest municipal affordable housing effort in the nation's history."

MIDDAGH STUDIO APARTMENTS

The people who lived in Middagh Studio Apartments, a Mitchell-Lama development in Brooklyn, were evicted when the owner exited the program. Various politicians were quoted in the press, claiming to have made herculean efforts to save them. I knew those politicians; I wanted to hear the real story. So one bitterly cold January night, I traveled to Brooklyn to meet with Anita Karl, who had been the Middagh tenant president. She and her husband were now living in a somewhat edgier neighborhood deeper in Brooklyn. We sat across a dining-room table with a tape recorder and some tortilla chips between us. Anita's striking wood sculptures hung on the walls.

A graceful, soft-spoken woman, Anita told me that her daughter had grown up at Middagh and didn't want her to talk about it anymore. "It was a terrible four-year ordeal. My daughter thinks it destroyed my health. I'm sure it has. You're never really quite over it."

"We moved there in 1977," she continued. "It was kind of a frontier area that had been designated for slum clearance. When the artists came, the area gradually became gentrified. Middagh was a little community, one of the few integrated buildings in Brooklyn Heights. People moved in when they were in their thirties and forties. Now they're in their sixties and seventies. Nobody had much money. Edward Penson, the owner, had homes in Boca Raton and out on Long Island. He thought of himself as a patron of the arts. He even opened a gallery in Soho." [Penson had acquired Middagh with all the usual Mitchell-Lama tax breaks, subsidies, and commitments to tenants.]

"Did any of the politicians or bureaucrats help you—anyone?"

"HPD told us, 'Don't worry about it; you're going to go into rent stabilization.' We believed them. They never told us that rent stabilization didn't apply to buildings occupied after 1973. Peter Vallone was the speaker of the Council. We found out later that he was just a spokesman for the real estate industry.[85]

"These people kept us in the lurch for a year, always holding out hope and saying vague things. It took us a while to realize that they were just going to leave us out to dry. We met with Vito Lopez, who was very slippery. We saw that pretty quickly."

"We got a smarmy letter from Dan Doctoroff. I went to a few of those borough president's task force meetings in Manhattan," Anita continued, "but they were a farce. I stopped going. Later, Lee Chong, the director, admitted that it was just a political front for the borough president. I went to Albany four times. I met twice with Joe Bruno's housing person. He was very polite. We learned that he was all for the landlords."

"What about the owners and their lawyers?"

"They were ruthless. The front doors were left unlocked; they turned off the heat from time to time. The hallways were filthy, and there were rodents running free. Cedric Turner didn't leave right away. His door was jackhammered off. I met him in the street after it was over. 'These people have made me homeless,' he told me. I never saw him after that."

After my meeting with Anita and her husband, I looked at a few of the newspaper accounts. Menachim Kastner, the owner's lawyer, was quoted in the local paper. He said "I don't believe that any doors were jackhammered off [apartments] that were in occupancy."

After the residents were evicted, there was a kinder and gentler phase. The new owners hired a former chairwoman of the Landmarks Preservation Commission. They were planning a large, luxury condominium on the site. She said:

We see [the Middagh conversion] as a transition between the lower scale of the townhouses and the higher scale of the towers outside of the district. We thought it would especially enhance the pedestrian streetscape.

She could talk the talk.

PHIPPS PLAZA

Sylvia Mendel was the tenant association president for Phipps Plaza, a Manhattan Mitchell-Lama development about the size of Independence Plaza. The owners announced that they were planning to exit the program. She had read about our fight at Independence Plaza and had participated in our rally at City Hall. She invited me to the legally mandated meeting in a large church where the landlord's lawyers and housing officials were going to explain things to the tenants.

When I walked in to the church, the city's housing officials were sitting up on a stage explaining in the most soothing language that the tenants were going to lose their homes. They didn't put it that way, of course, but that was the bottom line and the tenants knew it. The lawyers didn't say much. They looked benign and smiled pleasantly as if to say: *This is routine, nothing to get excited about, just a legal process.*

Tenants came up to the microphone in the center aisle of the church: "How the hell is this even possible?" "Why didn't anyone ever mention it when we moved in?" "We have our kids in school here." And so on. Some raised their voices; they were taking things personally! Security guards ringed the aisles.

There were the usual lawsuits; but a few months later, the owners took Phipps Plaza out of the Mitchell-Lama program and changed its name to "Kips Bay Court." They doubled the rents immediately and went up from there.

Tom "T-Bone" Stinson, a jazz pianist, ended up jumping off the Phipps Plaza roof. He couldn't make the rent. He had other problems too, but his estranged wife told reporters that the thing he was most depressed about was losing his apartment.

It's hard for those who haven't experienced the emotions that tenants feel when they learn that their rents are going to double. Some feel the tenants don't "own" their apartments anyway. The fact is that, in New York at least, tenants have few or no options. Most people live in apartments. It's home. A notice that your rent suddenly will double engenders the same sense of rage, despair, and betrayal that uninformed homeowners feel when the foreclosure notice is served because the variable-interest mortgage that they didn't understand kicked in. When the government sides with the banker in a black suit holding the legal papers, the villain whom audiences hissed at in the days of silent movies, they get angry at the government. The landlords and bankers stoke those fires, or, as with Mike, pit regulated tenants against those who want their homes: "What about the people who can afford to pay the new rents? What about them?"

Adam Weinstein, president of Phipps Plaza's non-profit ownership entity, told reporters that the tenants got a good deal: "I think I can say with good conscience that the rents we are offering are equivalent to the city's affordable housing program."[86] Weinstein didn't have much of a sense of irony. A few months later, I saw him on a local TV program. He was talking about the city's need for more affordable housing. He was earnest and convincing.[87]

This is how Mike's handlers describe his approach to Mitchell-Lama:

Mike is also protecting existing affordable housing and improving housing conditions. His administration has brought tenants and landlords together to keep more than 21,000 apartments from exiting the Mitchell-Lama program, one of the most effective middle-class housing programs in the city's history.[88]

Mike's New Housing Marketplace Plan is more than three-quarters completed. He says it will house 500,000 people by 2014. "That's more people than live in Miami," he said recently. Not only is he creating housing for "low-and medium-income families," but, "through our New Housing Marketplace Plan ... we've also created 120,000 jobs." And you don't have to take Mike's word for it: "I applaud Mayor Bloomberg and the hard-working teams at HPD and HDC on the unprecedented success of the New Housing Marketplace Plan," says Assemblyman Vito Lopez, Chairman of the Assembly Housing Committee.

Mike's Homeless Policies

The episodes I've described embody Mike's middle-class housing approach: relentless bullshit about protecting teachers, nurses, firefighters, and all those other salt-of-the-earth New Yorkers, all the while helping the real estate operators push them out of their homes. When it comes to homeless people who don't have many supporters, the iron fist comes out of the velvet glove. He once told attendees at a Working Families Party forum that the reason that shelter occupancy rates have reached record levels is that he has made city shelters "more attractive"! One of Mike's first attractive shelters was an unused Bronx jail that Rudy Giuliani had rejected as a shelter. The levels of peeling lead paint were eight times the toxicity level defined by the city's Health Department.

Mike began filling the old jail with homeless families, 90 to begin with. A firestorm of criticism erupted. Mike said he'd compromise and stop sending children younger than six years old to the jail. The courts finally ordered him to close it down.

He has herded homeless people into apartments with rats, water leaks, mold, and collapsed ceilings and floors. Many of them lack heat, hot water, electricity, or locks on the doors—and some have lead paint known to cause brain damage in small children.[89] Homeless people have various nicknames for these places, like "Cockroach City" and "Hotel Hell." No worries: Before the city enters into a contract, the landlord must promise to fix whatever is wrong.

The Coalition for the Homeless reported that a record 113,553 homeless people—including 42,888 children—slept in city-funded shelters in 2010, a 37 percent increase from 2002. The number of homeless families is 45 percent higher than when Mike took office.

More recently, Mike has ratcheted up his Dickensian approach to poor people. Here is the introduction to the most recent report, *Unhinged From Reality*, prepared by the Coalition for the Homeless:

> *Since November, Bloomberg administration officials have struggled to sell the fantastical notion that New Yorkers with genuine, viable housing options are rushing en masse to the Bellevue Men's Shelter, the Bedford-Atlantic Armory, the 1,000-bed Wards Island shelter complex, and similar warehouse-style facilities in order to sleep on metal cots and thin mattresses constructed by prison labor, in dormitories with upwards of 100 homeless adults in rows of identical cots three feet apart. And that these New Yorkers will spend months in the municipal shelter system, living in the same grim institutional conditions and eating the same grim institutional food, all while they actually have other housing available to them.[90]*

At this writing, a state court has blocked the imposition of Mike's new regulations that throw up additional hurdles for people who need shelter.

Former Homeless Services Commissioner Robert Hess, when questioned about the administration's approach to homelessness, said, "I don't know anybody who can develop the perfect program."

Hess resigned in 2010. Seth Diamond replaced him. The Coalition for the Homeless was concerned "that at a time of double digit unemployment and record breaking family homelessness the Bloomberg administration is turning to someone who seems to see homelessness more as a character flaw instead of the inevitable result of low wages, no jobs, and high rents."

The Mayor's Fund to Advance New York City has initiated various antipoverty pilot programs and begun exporting them to other cities (along with the homeless themselves, who he pays to leave town). Glenn Pasanen, who teaches political science at Lehman College, has been reporting on these issues for the *Gotham Gazette* since 2001. He observes:

> [Bloomberg's] much-heralded private efforts have had little to no effect on poverty in New York and seem unlikely to have any significant impact in the future. Many are modeled on programs in developing countries like Mexico, Colombia, and Bangladesh. ... They have been extensively researched; two recent surveys offer little evidence that such tactics might help the poor in urban America.

Mike: *Colombia? Bangladesh? Give me your tired, your poor, your huddled masses yearning to breathe free. I know what to do with them.*

CHAPTER TWO

Mike, the
Education Mayor

◄○►

Mike didn't know anything about education, but he was determined to be the "Education Mayor."[91] George H.W. Bush had been the "Education President" and Junior was "No Child Left Behind." The Bushes didn't know anything about education either. Mike would show those knuckleheads how a real CEO got things done.

In 2002, Albany gave him full control of the public schools. For chancellor he chose Joel Klein, an antitrust lawyer who had attended New York public schools and had once taught a sixth-grade math class. Lacking education credentials, Klein would need a waiver from the state education department. "If the scholarship and background requirements that Joel Klein has doesn't [*sic*] pass," the mayor said, "nobody would pass." Klein got his waiver and Mike and Joel went to work.

They grew the city's annual education budget from $12.7 billion to $23 billion. The bureaucracy grew by 40 percent. Twenty-two administrators were paid more than $180,000 a year. The public relations staff grew from five to twenty-three. A questionable reading program called Month-by-Month Phonics was made mandatory in 1,000 city schools. Mike called the new approach Children First.

◄◦►

Klein imposed central control over the entire system, including the curriculum and teaching methods. Sol Stern, a senior fellow at the conservative Manhattan Institute and a serious scholar, had supported Mike's takeover of the school system. He had seen enough. In April 2003, he wrote:

> *Unless Bloomberg and his handpicked schools chancellor, Joel Klein, admit to some monumental blunders, discredited progressive methods for the teaching of the three Rs such as "whole language," "writing process," and "fuzzy math" will soon be enforced in every single classroom in 1,000 New York City schools. This is a disaster in the making.*

Stern didn't know that Mike was a graduate of the "never apologize, never explain" school of management and politics. He reported that school administrators "were warned to shut up if they have any complaints about the curriculum shift. I tried to talk to several of the principals, but met with an almost blanket refusal to comment. One principal who did speak begged me not to mention his name or his school." It was vintage Mike: *Get the numbers up and keep your mouth shut.*

By 2005, no-bid contracts in the schools had soared to $120 million from $693,000 in Giuliani's last year. Consultants always know who signs the paychecks; they climbed over each other to praise Mike and his chancellor. But the education needle hadn't budged. It would take a miracle to demonstrate measurable improvements before the November election. Mike served one up. Stern, whose own kids attended public schools, reported on Mike's Bronx Miracle.

A few months before the 2005 mayoral election, Mike bused reporters to P.S. 33, a poor, predominantly minority school in the Bronx, to watch him congratulate the children, teachers, and principal, Elba Lopez-Spangenberg, on the astounding one-year gain of almost 50 percentage points on a fourth-grade reading test, to just four points below the average for the state's richest suburban districts. Front-page headlines the next day hailed the "historic gains." The principal got a $15,000 bonus that raised her annual pension about $10,000 a year, and she retired. The newspapers pumped up the P.S. 33 results. If the naysayers needed proof that Mike was turning the public schools around, there it was.

The 2005 mayoral campaign featured the new affordable housing plan, the Bronx Miracle, and all the other things Mike was doing for nurses, teachers, and firefighters. He even paid another visit to Israel, telling the *New York Times*, "Religion, I'm not comfortable in talking about .... It may be good politics, but it's not me."[92] That was for the *Times* secularists. His Orthodox Jewish amanuensis, city councilman Simcha Felder, came along on the trip. He had a different sort of message to assure Orthodox Jewish voters: "When you speak to him personally, in casual conversation, you hear a lot more about his Jewishness."

The *New York Times* fretted that Mike's outsized spending advantage—he would outspend Ferrer by 10 to 1—"can undermine the election process." It then endorsed him. Fernando Ferrer was crushed beneath another free and paid media blitz.

When the 2006 education test scores came out, the same P.S. 33 students, who were now fifth graders, had dropped back to a pass rate of 41 percent on their reading tests. As Stern observed, "In 2005 they shone as stars of a mayoral campaign. In 2006 they were truly 'left behind.'"

Pressed by reporters and outraged parents, Klein launched an "investigation." Three years later the Department of Education concluded that there had been no evidence of cheating. Klein investigating Klein, his sleuths never questioning Lopez or the students in that fourth-grade class until they were in the eighth grade. The answer sheets had already been destroyed.

Safely back in City Hall, Mike reversed course and decentralized again. Schools would be graded from A to F. If students performed well, principals and teachers would be rewarded with hard cash. If they didn't, the schools could be closed, the principals could start looking for work, and the teachers might be relegated to the infamous (now abandoned) "rubber rooms"—more politely "reassignment centers." Soon Mike and Joel announced another miracle: 77 percent of the schools that received an F in 2007 got an A or B in 2008. In one year!

To achieve this miracle, tests were made easier to pass, teachers taught to the tests, poor students were discouraged or excluded from taking them, and minimum passing scores were lowered. Teachers even changed students' answers.

NYU professor Diane Ravitch, a leading authority on New York City public schools—also an early supporter of mayoral control—had been writing for several years that the state tests were dumbed down and the scores were bogus. She complained that the mayor and the chancellor "are trying to intimidate me, and they're trying to silence me, and I'm not going to be silenced." She wouldn't be silenced but her voice and the voices of other critics could be drowned out. The entire country was hearing about *The Greatest Improvements in Public Education the Country Has Ever Seen!*

Finally, on November 15, 2007, the federal government released the scores of 11 urban districts that had participated in the National Assessment of Educational Progress (NAEP), the gold standard for measuring student achievement on a national basis.

After five years of *who you gonna believe, Mike or your own lyin' eyes?* the *New York Times* published a front-page piece: "Little Progress for City Schools on National Test: Racial Gap Continues; Contrast with Results Seen on State Exams Under Bloomberg."

> *New York City's eighth graders have made no significant progress in reading and math since Mayor Michael R. Bloomberg took control of the city schools, according to federal test scores released yesterday, in contrast with the largely steady gains that have been recorded on state tests. The national scores also showed little narrowing of the achievement gap between white students and their black and Hispanic counterparts.*[93]

New York was one of only two out of ten cities in which the percentage of students performing at or above "basic" in eighth-grade reading actually declined between 2003 and 2007. Jennifer Medina, the *Times* reporter, wrote that Mike had "trumpeted improving state test scores as evidence that the city is setting the pace for urban school reform," but the federal scores "suggest that the city's gains are limited. The most significant increase in fourth-grade reading scores occurred in 2002, before Mr. Bloomberg took control."

Joel Klein said he "saw plenty of good news in the federal scores" and immediately issued a press release headlined "New York City Public School Students Make Gains on 2007 National Assessment of Educational Progress (NAEP) Tests."

In 2009, under a new Board of Regents chancellor and state education commissioner, the tests were revised. In 2010, the new scores were released. More than half the city's public school students failed the English exams, and only 54 percent passed math.

"This doesn't mean the kids did any worse—quite the contrary," Mike told *NBC News'* Education Nation Summit. "What this is simply saying is that we've redefined what our objectives are for the kids."

In March 2010, *Times* reporter Jennifer Medina wrote another piece, headlined "Another Rise in City Pupils Graduating in Four Years." Medina wrote that the mayor appeared jubilant at the news conference, as he "jumped enthusiastically from one chart to the next, Mr. Bloomberg emphasized that the city was outpacing the rest of the state in graduation rate improvements. ... The job will never be done, but we're on the right track. ... The results for New York City are historic," he said. "If this doesn't put a smile on everybody in New York's face, I don't know what will."[94]

Few who understood education policy thought there had been any improvements. Mike and Joel had found creative ways to make the numbers come out right.

If graduation rates were going to be the headline number, then playing with the discharge rates could force them up. Between the graduating high school classes of 2000 and 2007, a total of 142,262 New York City students were discharged. None was counted as a dropout, and all were excluded from the graduation rate calculations. When two-thirds or more of the graduates taking basic City University of New York placement tests—for community colleges—fail, what do graduation rates mean anyway?

David C. Bloomfield of the Manhattan Institute, another supporter-turned-critic, sums up Mike's record this way:

The [DOE] website is a perfect example of what makes everyone so mad about the way the Mayor has handled the schools: data manipulation, grandiose claims, and almost no way to find out that a third (or is it more?) of our schools are failing under No Child Left Behind.[95]

◄○►

As for narrowing the ethnic achievement gap, Mike gave a talk at the NBC Education Nation Summit in 2010. After citing the dismal national record, he said:

Here in New York City we've spent the last eight years transforming a broken and dysfunctional school system and reversing decades of educational neglect. ... Our African-American and Hispanic students have closed the ethnic achievement gap on state tests by 37 percent in reading, and 18 percent in math. The improvement for Hispanic students is the most dramatic success story.

But the national scores showed that eighth-grade reading levels for black, Hispanic, and lower-income students fell more in New York than in any other urban district.

Gordon Macinnes, a fellow at the Century Foundation, is a serious education scholar.[96] He applauded the "New York State Chancellor Meryl Tisch and Commissioner of Education Joseph Steiner "for laying bare the deception and softness of state standards and testing. ... New York ends the fantasy about swift and dramatic gains in student achievement." Not surprisingly, the consequences are most severe for low-income, black, and Latino students:

The percentage of economically disadvantaged students in grades three through eight scoring "proficient" or above declined precipitously—from 66.9 percent in 2009 to 39.1 percent in 2010. The percentage of English learners below "basic" more than quadrupled that year, to 39.4 percent, while the percentage of black students scoring proficient or better tumbled from 64.3 to 34.4 percent. The decline was steepest for students in charter schools, where those scoring proficient or better slumped from 76.1 to 43 percent.[97]

Most observers who had supported mayoral control have long ago penetrated the fog, but Mike is still serving up the same stew pot of payoffs and propaganda.

Before Klein left his post in 2010, appropriately to join Rupert Murdoch's organization to sell education products to school systems, he made a presentation to the press. He "found much to be excited about in the performance of black students."

"Whose blacks are on top?" Klein enthused, pointing to a chart showing that black fourth graders were performing better than those in the rest of the state and in the nation. "While I would like to see more gap closure, I nevertheless think in a rising tide where people are doing better—and our blacks are dramatically outperforming everybody else here—I think that's a good story."

"Whose blacks? Our blacks." That *is* a good story.

Send in the Clowns

In November 2010, Mike replaced Klein with Hearst magazine executive Cathie Black, a member of Mike's social circle and a good friend of his long-time companion, Diana Taylor.

Except for the fact that she had had one, Black didn't know anything about education either. Parents were in an uproar. Mike had a ready sports metaphor for the naysayers: "We had a great pitcher the first seven innings. Cathie Black is the right closer to bring in." Mike muscled through a waiver of the qualification rules and Black set out to show parents that she had the common touch. When they asked her what ideas she had about overcrowded classrooms, she said, "Could we just have some birth control for a while? It could really help us all out a lot." Ha, ha. Clearly, Black was Mike's kind of gal. The parents weren't laughing, though. She called the decisions about classroom space "Sophie's choices," a reference to William Styron's novel about a mother forced to choose which one of her children would live and which would die in Auschwitz.

Parents just couldn't relate to Black's sense of humor. Gallantly, Mike defended her: "Cathie Black made a joke," he told reporters. "Some people took it the wrong way. She apologized. ... I picked the right person. She'll try to fulfill the dream that Martin Luther King had for everybody." Black resigned abruptly in April 2011.

Send in the Cops

Mike has been invoking the legacy of Martin Luther King, Jr. since his earliest days in office. He has expanded the Giuliani-initiated police presence in the city's deeply segregated public schools to more than 200 armed and uniformed NYPD officers and more than 5,000 school safety officers who wear police uniforms and have full arrest powers.[98] There are more police and safety officers patrolling New York City schools than the entire police forces in Washington, D.C., Detroit, Boston, Baltimore, Dallas, Phoenix, San Francisco, San Diego or Las Vegas. The city's public schools are patrolled by the fifth-largest police force in the country.

They roam the schools unaccountable to and unrestrained by school administrators. After years of horrific press accounts and parental complaints of physical abuse, the New York Civil Liberties Union and the ACLU Foundation brought Michael Bloomberg, Ray Kelly, and various other officials to court. Joshua Colangelo-Bryan, the co-counsel on the case, told of the 11-year-old who was "handcuffed and perp-walked into a police precinct for doing nothing more than doodling on a desk in erasable ink. Amazingly, no one in the police department or the school seemed to think there was anything wrong with that."

The lawyer wasn't describing an isolated doodling incident involving the arrest of a pre-teen student. Four- and five-year-old kids are taken away in handcuffs. The federal complaint recounts case after case of students charged with minor breaches of discipline who are handcuffed, locked in seclusion rooms, taken to police precincts, and even transported to hospitals for psychiatric evaluations. Uniformed thugs under colorable claims of legal authority are doing serious damage to young kids, and they doing it on their own terms—without having to consult with teachers or school administrators, let alone parents.

The massive police presence is unlike that in any public school system the country has ever known. Stories of sadistic abuse are common. Because people seem unable to grasp the enormity of these crimes, and because numbers are bloodless abstractions that don't evoke the nightmarish conditions, I've set forth some of these stories. Mindful that some are allegations in a complaint—although many incidents have resulted in money judgments against the city—there is a pattern to them that can't be dismissed. And even if one were inclined to the view that these are difficult kids, the unrestrained violence and the ratcheting up of minor infractions into full-blown arrest and imprisonment episodes are inexcusable, the absence of accountability even more so. It means that the behavior is condoned, if not encouraged. This is a system in deep crisis.

The Stories

On October 9, 2007, a student at East Side Community High School in Manhattan tried to enter school early to catch up on schoolwork. A School Safety Officer refused her entry. They argued. He arrested her and paraded her in handcuffs out of the school's main entrance. The school principal insisted she be taken out of a side entrance so as not to disrupt the school and unnecessarily humiliate the girl. The officer arrested the principal and charged him with obstruction of governmental administration and resisting arrest! A judge later dismissed the charges.

◄o►

In March 2009, M.M., a 6th grader at Hunts Point School, was drawing on paper during class. Her friend reached over to her desk and drew on her paper. Playfully, she drew on his, and then they both drew a line on each other's desks with erasable markers: 6th graders making mischief. Their teacher told them to erase the marks immediately. They got up to get tissues. But safety officers arrived first and took them to the security office where they were interrogated. "You know that's graffiti, right?" M.M. explained that she had planned to erase the marks but didn't have the opportunity.

They put her in handcuffs and marched her back to the classroom to get her jacket and book bag. She said the handcuffs were hurting her, and asked that they be loosened. They refused. The frightened girl asked for her mother and started to cry. They told her to remove her shoes and sweater for a pat-down search. Then they took both doodlers in handcuffs to the police precinct where M.M.'s mother was waiting. She saw her daughter being brought into the precinct in handcuffs, her jacket falling off, her shoelaces untied, hair ruffled, and crying, "Mommy get me out of here." They were fingerprinted, photographed, and handcuffed to a bench.

The police officer threatened to put them in with the general jail population, whom he described as "killers" and "murderers." "You are going to have to scream and you'll be lucky if anyone comes to help you." "You scared, you scared?"

M.M. is scared. She won't be doodling anymore.

—◄o►—

D.Y. is thirteen years old and enrolled in the 8th grade at the Lou Gehrig School in the Bronx. At around 8:30 a.m. on October 7, 2009, her mother dropped her and her girlfriends across the street from the school. As the three girls were approaching the school entrance, two adults approached and began threatening them. The frightened girl sent her mother a text message to come back.

A school safety officer observed the exchange and instructed the girls and the two strangers to go into the school building. The strangers entered the building, but the girls were afraid to follow them. D.Y. said that she wanted to wait for her mother, whereupon the officer grabbed her arms and called for "back-up."

The officers pushed her face into a gate, put her arms behind her back, and handcuffed her. As they entered the school building, one safety officer put her foot out, tripping the girl. She fell stomach first onto the floor. The officer put her knee on D.Y.'s back and yelled at her to "get up." Eventually, she was let up and taken to the security office, where they threw her into a chair in handcuffs. Her mother was finally allowed to take her home. The school safety officers continue to harass and intimidate her. D.Y. is scared they will arrest her on trumped-up charges.

—◄o►—

On January 18, 2007, A.M., a fifteen-year-old 10th grader, was staying late in her classroom to complete a final exam. As she exited the classroom to go to the cafeteria for the lunch period, a safety officer stopped her and instructed her to use an alternate stairwell. She complied, turning around and using the other stairwell.

On the second floor, a school official stopped her and told her to go to the detention room because she was not supposed to be in the hallways. She explained that she had just finished a final exam, but complied with the order and began to walk toward the detention room. An officer, who had been watching the conversation, approached her from behind, grabbed her book bag, and yelled at her to go to the detention room. He pushed her.

She asked for his badge number. He threatened to lock her up, twisted her arm behind her back, handcuffed her, and pushed her face against the wall. He took her away in handcuffs through the hallways to the dean's office, where her belongings were searched.

She had been injured and was taken to a hospital for treatment, after which she was taken to the local police precinct, placed in a back room, and handcuffed to a pole. Eventually she was released. She transferred to another public school.

◄o►

In the fall of 2008, a safety officer kicked in the door to a bathroom stall occupied by S.C., a seventeen-year-old student enrolled in the 12th grade at Robert F. Kennedy High School in Queens. The boy was hit in the head and bleeding. The officer told him, "That's life. It will stop bleeding." The boy reported the incident to the school principal, who told him there was nothing he could do about it. The boy's father went to the local precinct to file a complaint. The precinct canceled both meetings they had scheduled with him. The safety officer was transferred to a middle school in the area. S.C.'s parents filed a civil suit against the City. It was settled for $55,500.

◄o►

C.S. was a freshman. Bobby pins in her hair activated the metal detector at the school's entrance. Three officers took her into a bathroom and instructed all the other girls to leave. She was subjected to an invasive search during which a metal detector wand was placed against her skin under her bra, purportedly to ensure that she was not hiding a razor, cell phone, or iPod between her bra and her body. "Every day I go to school and I face being harassed, pushed, shoved, yelled at, disrespected and illegally searched," she said. "All they implement is fear."

◄o►

Nancy Rosenbloom, an attorney for the Legal Aid Society, testified before the New York City Council that a student client—a small twelve-year old girl—was arrested for allegedly assaulting a large, male school safety officer. The juvenile court judge heard testimony and reviewed the videotape showing that the officer was the initial aggressor. The judge dismissed all charges.

Rosenbloom testified that her office had defended another child accused of assaulting a school safety officer. The charges were dismissed after a videotape showed that several school safety officers had initiated the altercation by pushing the student into a corner, hitting him, and then laughing.

—◄○►—

Tara Foster, an attorney with the Queens Legal Services, testified that she had defended a student charged with striking a safety officer. Witnesses testified that the officer initiated the altercation, pushing her against the wall, grabbing her by the hair, dragging her, and punching her in the head. He stomped on the cell phone of a witness who attempted to videotape the incident. The school disciplinary charges against the student were dismissed. The officer wasn't punished.

—◄○►—

C.R. was sixteen years old and enrolled in Samuel Gompers High School in the Bronx. Safety officers took him out of the classroom for talking too much. They threw him against the wall, jumped on him when he fell to the ground, and hand-cuffed him. He was taken to the hospital where his head was stitched up. They charged him with assault, resisting arrest, and harassment. The City settled the subsequent lawsuit for $39,000.

—◄○►—

J.G. was enrolled in the High School of Fashion Industries in Manhattan. He filed a lawsuit, *Gonzalez v. City of New York*, No. 116093-07 (N.Y. Sup. Ct. filed Nov. 20, 2007), alleging that he was stopped for being in the hallway without a pass. Six safety officers threw him to the ground and beat him, resulting in a fracture to his left hand that required surgery. He had multiple bruises around his head, neck, and shoulders, and other physical injuries.

The *New York Daily News* reported on June 19, 2008, that an NYPD school safety officer handcuffed a five-year-old boy and transported him to a psychiatric hospital, after the boy threw what was described as a "temper tantrum." On March 10, 2008, the *New York Daily News* reported that a NYPD school safety officer handcuffed two four-year-old boys for refusing to take a nap.

Between 2002 and 2007, the police received 2,670 complaints against school safety officers, resulting in an average of 500 per year, or one complaint for every eight to ten school safety officers per year. Twenty-seven percent of those complaints were substantiated. In 2008, there were 1,159 complaints, a staggering rate of almost one complaint for every four school safety officers employed. Fifteen percent of these complaints alleged excessive force, abuse of authority, discourtesy, or offensive language by school safety officers.

On November 29 and 30, 2006, police vehicles pulled up to the Community School for Social Justice and the Health Opportunities High School in the Bronx. The NYPD was bringing in its roving metal detectors. Approximately 150 students attend the two schools. About 40 school safety agents swarmed around the building, screaming at students to empty their pockets and remove their belts, hairclips, and bracelets. They cut off students who tried to enter school through alternate entrances, yelling "Round them up!" and chasing down those who tried to leave.

They searched backpacks and confiscated cell phones, iPods, food, metal-studded belts, nail files, perfume, hand sanitizer, loose change, CD players, and other "weapons."

Girls were searched by male officers. After being pushed against the wall for frisking, many were subjected to intrusive searches with handheld metal detectors.

One girl was forced to squat while a male officer repeatedly traced his handheld metal detector up her inner thigh until it beeped on the button of her jeans. The frightened girl repeated that there was nothing in her jeans, but he kept at it, making her fear a cavity search, until he finally let her go.

"After the metal detectors came in, I felt like this was a different school," twelfth-grader Brian said. "It just doesn't feel right anymore."

◄◦►

On February 3, 2005, safety officer Juan Gonzalez barged into a classroom to arrest a Bronx Guild High School student. He said she had been cursing in the hallway. Gonzalez hadn't consulted the school's principal, Michael Soguero, as regulations required.

Soguero was called. He asked Gonzalez to leave. Gonzalez tried to grab the female student. Soguero intervened. Gonzalez arrested him!

James Burgos, a school aide, tried to intervene. He was arrested. The principal and the aide spent the night in jail. The student spent two nights in jail. Criminal charges were pressed against all three. Soguero and Burgos were removed from their positions. They were reinstated when the charges were dropped more than two months later. The student was "encouraged" to transfer to a different school.

"Using profanity, I'm not supposed to suspend a child for that," Soguero said later. "Yet an officer can issue a summons for that and even put a child in cuffs and call it disorderly conduct." That a "safety officer" can behave this way and have a principal put in jail speaks volumes about the culture and management of the city's public schools.

◄◦►

On March 8, 2005, at least seven NYPD officers arrived at the New School for Arts and Sciences in the Bronx after teachers called 911 to ask for medical assistance for a student who had been involved in a fight. Before they arrived, Cara Wolfson-Kronen, a social studies teacher, called the 911 operator to report that several teachers had stopped the fight and controlled the situation, and things were peaceful again.

The police arrived anyway. One of them demanded that the teachers identify the students. Quinn Kronen, an English teacher and Cara's husband, said the students were now peacefully sitting in the classroom. One cop yelled at her, "You fucking teachers need to get your shit together. These kids are running crazy. You need to get rid of them."

When Quinn Kronen objected to the profanity, a Sergeant Walter responded "You better shut the fuck up" or she would arrest him. Cara Wolfson-Kronen objected. Walter said: "That's it; cuff the bitch." She was taken out of the school in handcuffs. For a little extra measure of punishment for speaking when told to shut up, they forced her to stand outside in subfreezing temperatures without a jacket. Police also arrested Quinn Kronen. The court dismissed the charges at their initial court hearing.

On March 22, 2005, the two teachers received an anonymous letter signed by "The Brotherhood." The letter threatened them with physical harm for "messing up with our fellow officers." It continued, "If I were you I'd be planning my getting out of New York fast." The teachers reported the letter. The case was referred to the Civilian Complaint Review Board and the Internal Affairs Bureau of the NYPD. In 2007, the City of New York paid $60,002 to settle a civil lawsuit brought by the two teachers.[99]

The Spin

Here's Mike at the NBC News Education Nation Summit.

We should never forget that every morning in this city—and all across our country—moms and dads wake up at 5:30 to prepare breakfast for their children. They dress and get them ready for school. They grab their little hands as they cross the street, they take them to our doorstep, and then they leave them in our trust. Their children are our future—and I work for them. And I make this promise to them and to their parents: We will work just as hard as you do to provide a better future for your children.

On January 12, 2012 Mike delivered his State of the City message at Morris High School in the Bronx:

CHAPTER THREE

Mike, the
Progressive Mayor

◄o►

On February 15, 2003, in cities around the world, millions of people took to the streets for a peaceful protest against the impending war with Iraq.[100] On orders from Mike, the NYPD refused to allow protesters to march past the United Nations—or anywhere else. He used the familiar 9-11 rationale. A federal judge upheld his position. The protesters were crowded into "pens"—metal barricades that formed closed areas. The city refused to allow portable restrooms; barking police dogs kept the people inside the pens.

The police told protestors they couldn't chant without a sound permit. They arrested people who photographed them. Cops shouted at women "FUCKING SCUMBAG!"; "FUCKING CUNT!"

Mounted police charged their horses into the crowds standing on the sidewalks. Police on foot chased, surrounded, and beat people as they lay on the pavement. One cop forced a young man to the ground and pushed him face down in horse manure while others piled on top of him. Three cops pummelled another man to the ground and beat him with fists and billy clubs. Police used pepper spray that caused prolonged, extreme eye pain.

Four cops roughly handcuffed an elderly man face down on the ground. He was a Presbyterian minister who had grabbed the bridle of a police horse as it was about to run into a woman with a small child. Virtually all of the approximately 350 people who were arrested were driven around the city for hours in handcuffs, in dark, unheated vans, with no food or water and no access to bathrooms or medical treatment. When they got to police headquarters, many were forced to stand outside in the freezing cold for an hour or more, handcuffed and chained together. They asked for lawyers and were ignored or threatened with prolonged detention. They were interrogated about their political and religious affiliations. Such was the peaceful protest against the Iraq war in New York.

The *New York Times* account conjured up an image of cops and demonstrators arm in arm singing *Kumbaya, My Lord.* The story emphasized public school children waving flags, Pete Seeger and Richie Havens singing songs, Harry Belafonte and Bishop Desmond Tutu making speeches, a festive event. The paper quoted Ray Kelly: "I think it went well. For the number of people here, it was orderly. The vast majority of people were cooperative." Not until the ninth paragraph was there a hint of the dark side.[101] The story line was that some protesters were aggressive and the police were restrained.

Elsewhere on that same day, cities all over the world accommodated large marches without any major incidents. Washington, D.C., with many high-risk locations, handled more than 100,000 protesters without a problem. That city has a total of about 4,000 cops—slightly more than one tenth of the NYPD's force—along with a few thousand federal police.

Mike stayed in the background during the New York protest. At the next one, he was front and center.

The 2004 Republican National Convention

Mike invited the Republicans to hold their 2004 national convention in New York.[102] He gave them $5 million in cash and another $2 million in legal and accounting services. Most New Yorkers would have given the Son of Sam higher approvals than the Bush–Cheney regime. Mike's invitation was his characteristic *fuck you, I'm in charge here.* His public stance was: "What's wrong with using my own money to further the city's agenda?" He told WNYC radio listeners that he'd be "spending the convention outside with the police to make sure the protesters have the ability to protest." He had rejected all 15 applications for permits for protest marches.

Fearing a repeat of the Iraq fiasco, the director of the New York Civil Liberties Union, Donna Lieberman, called on the administration to "ensure that police officers refrain from the use of force—including the use of horses, pepper spray, or other instruments of force." Apparently resigned to the police practice of penning in protesters, she asked that the pens have "openings sufficient to permit people to enter and exit freely."

This time the police arrested some 1,800 people, the vast majority of whom were peaceful demonstrators. Some were bystanders who were trapped when police corralled crowds with orange plastic nets. There were beatings and prolonged detentions in an old bus garage with oil, asbestos, and other toxic materials on the floor. "It's not supposed to be Club Med," Mike said.

Ray Kelly said, "The Republican National Convention was perhaps the finest hour in the history of the New York City Police Department."

A court-ordered release of NYPD documents revealed that the arrest, detention, fingerprinting, and interrogation of demonstrators were all part of the pre-convention planning process. For at least a year, an "RNC Intelligence Squad" had been infiltrating churches and antiwar, antiglobalization, and environmental groups. At the convention, undercover agents became provocateurs, stirring up disorderly protests.

More recently, the NYPD blocked reporters from viewing its sweep of Occupy Wall Street. It grounded the news helicopters and took away press passes.[103] Mike said, "NYPD routinely keeps press off to the side to prevent the situation from getting worse. It's to protect the press."

The increasingly menacing NYPD presence at political protests gives white people a taste of what goes on every day in poor neighborhoods of color where the police engage in a so-called zero-tolerance policing regime grounded in the idea that signs of disorder, such as broken windows, graffiti, and the like, signify a breakdown of the social fabric and encourage more serious crime. Most people agree that getting rid of graffiti, squeegee men, and other signs of social disorder are good things, but systematic abuse by the NYPD out of sight of reporters, cameras, and white New Yorkers is a well-documented and growing phenomenon. It is, in fact, a city policy.

Marijuana

Before his first election Mike was asked whether he had ever smoked marijuana. "You bet I did!" he grinned. "And I enjoyed it." Some have suggested that it wasn't true, that candidate Mike was currying favor with the reporters who were covering him, either because he was presenting himself as a candid person or maybe because reporters smoke pot. Earlier in this account I chose to take him at his word because it was a convenient device to tell the tongue-in-cheek story of how he came to the idea of establishing Bloomberg LP.

Does Mike smoke pot? It doesn't matter. Once he became Mayor Mike, he turned New York into the world's marijuana arrest capital, and those arrests have been aimed almost exclusively at young black and Hispanic males.

In his first nine years in office, the NYPD made almost 350,000 arrests for pot possession, far more than Koch, Giuliani, and Dinkins combined. The vast majority of sworn police statements that support the arrests are false, and everyone involved in the criminal justice system knows it.

Since 1977, simple possession of a small amount of marijuana (less than seven-eighths of an ounce) has been the equivalent of a traffic violation. For possession to become a misdemeanor, the marijuana must be burning or open to public view. Why then is misdemeanor marijuana possession charged more than any other offense in New York City, while possession as a violation is hardly ever charged? That's one question.

Second, at least one study has found that whites between the ages of 18 and 25 use marijuana more frequently than blacks, but more than half of the people arrested for marijuana possession in New York City are black and about one third are Hispanic. What's going on? Are tens of thousands of young black and Hispanic kids walking around the streets smoking pot in plain view?

"There is no defense for this policy," wrote *New York Times* columnist Bob Herbert. "It's a gruesome, racist practice that should offend all New Yorkers, and it should cease." Needless to say, Mike and Ray Kelly don't much care what Bob Herbert thinks.

Targeting young black and Hispanic males isn't new. As always with this mayor, it's the scale that's unprecedented. In 2011, police stopped and questioned people 684,330 times, a 14 percent increase over 2010 and a roughly 600 percent increase from a decade ago. Eighty-seven percent of those stopped were black or Hispanic.

The cops (illegally) order them to empty their pockets. If they are carrying marijuana it is "in public view." It's as simple as that.[104] From 2004 through 2010, approximately 3 million young people were subjected to police stops, frisks, and street interrogations. According to the NYPD's own reports, nearly nine out of ten were completely innocent. Hundreds of thousands of innocent kids are put through the arrest–jail–criminal court meat grinder, yet there is barely a peep from the black and Hispanic clergymen–politicians. "You bet I did, and I enjoyed it!"

—◀○▶—

And here's the topper: Mike has launched another "pioneering new initiative." He calls this one his Young Men's Initiative.

His adviser, Andrea Batista Schlesinger, explains:

It was the Mayor's frustration with the involvement of young black and Latino males in the criminal-justice system that sparked this entire effort. Is the Young Men's Initiative controversial? Sure. Any discussion of the intersection of race, class, and gender will arouse emotion. That's why most political leaders shy away from it. Thankfully for the black and Latino males of New York City, Mayor Bloomberg isn't one of them.[105]

The *New York Times* put the good news on the front page of the Metro section: "Bloomberg to Use Own Funds in Plan to Aid Minority Youth."[106]

"Mike didn't just issue a report, or wag his finger," Schlesinger gushed. "He told the city agencies that interact with young men of color to put a stop to disparities. He put his money where his mouth is with an unprecedented $127 million funding commitment, donating $30 million personally."

—◄o►—

After four years of litigation and court rulings that were largely ignored, on October 5, 2011 a federal court appointed a monitor to oversee the city's fire department, which is 97 percent white. The ruling was accompanied by a court opinion that said, "The evidence adduced in this case gives the court little hope that Mayor Michael R. Bloomberg or any of his senior leadership has any intention of stepping up to the task of ending discrimination at the F.D.N.Y."

The court went on to note, "Instead of facing hard facts and asking hard questions about the city's abysmal track record of hiring black and Hispanic firefighters, the Bloomberg administration dug in and fought back."

Mike held a press conference the same day in which he said he had launched "the most successful and most diverse recruitment campaign in the history of the F.D.N.Y. ... The judge was not elected to run the city, and you can rest assured that we'll be in court for a long time."[107]

Operation Impact

No law requires people to carry identification and produce it on demand of the police. But if you're young, black, or Hispanic, there is such a law—street law. That's why Mike wants "New Yorkers [read black and Hispanic] to understand the importance of obtaining ID and [the Young Men's Initiative] will be helping them to do it."

"Operation Impact" is a project that floods poor, minority neighborhoods with rookie cops who make arrests to meet quotas. Young black and Hispanic males who don't carry identification are routinely arrested, charged with misdemeanor trespass, and locked up overnight. Sometimes they are arrested in their own buildings where they fail to produce identification.

Recently, a young white college student was on the wrong end of the no-identification, arrest, and jail process. *New York Times* columnist Jim Dwyer reported the following episode.

On October 22, 2011, a 21-year-old girl and a male friend were walking in Riverside Park after closing time. They were part of a group of visiting Carnegie Mellon University students.

They didn't know there was a curfew for walking in the park. Cops pulled up in police cars, ticketed the male for trespassing and allowed him to leave when he showed his identification. The girl had left her wallet in the nearby hotel and asked if someone could bring it to the scene. Too late for that.

Dwyer wrote that the young woman was handcuffed and moved around the city from the station house on West 126th Street to central booking in Lower Manhattan and then back to Harlem, and then back downtown for booking, where she spent a second night in custody.

The case was dismissed when she finally got before a judge.

Dwyer commented on the marijuana arrest practice:

Here, in the pointless arrest of Ms. Zucker, is a crime that is not even on the books: the staggering waste of spirit, the squandering of public resources, the follies disguised as crime-fighting. About 40,000 people a year—the vast majority of them young black and Latino men—are fed like widgets onto a conveyor belt of arrest, booking and court, after being told to empty their pockets and thus commit the misdemeanor of "open display" of marijuana.[108]

A former corrections commissioner described being locked up overnight in one of these facilities:

It's debasing, it's difficult. You're probably in a fairly gross police lockup. You probably have no toilet paper. You're given a baloney sandwich, and the baloney is green.[109]

When the defendant is brought before a judge, usually the next day, he almost always pleads guilty and goes home. If he refuses to plead, he's bogged down in the court system for months, with repeated adjournments, time lost from school or a job, and an uncertain outcome. He goes home with a lifelong criminal record.

Affected communities are keenly aware of the abuses, of course. They're torn between the need for police protection and rage at the NYPD's arrogance and lawlessness. But if you don't live in one of those communities, and if all you read is that New York is the "safest large city in America" and "our innovative efforts to reduce crime and increase New Yorkers' quality of life are working," and you watch Ray Kelly on television talking to Charlie Rose about how appreciative these communities are, well then everything's fine, especially when a progressive mayor is spending his own money on young men's initiatives.

—◄○►—

It's only a small exaggeration to say that if they make their quotas, cops are immune from punishment as to how they make them.

In 2001, there were 4,260 cases of police misconduct brought into the Civilian Complaint Review Board. In 2009, there were 7,664. Reported cases are of course only a small fraction of what happens on the streets, and only a small fraction of those cases (in 2009, less than 4 percent) are forwarded to the NYPD for action.[110]

The police commissioner has the sole discretion to impose discipline. Even after they've survived the procedural strainer, about half the cases that reach Kelly's desk end with no action taken. But if you're a cop with a conscience, watch out.

Woe unto the Whistle Blowers

Adrian Schoolcraft, a young cop, complained to his supervisors about the faked summonses and stop-and-frisk reports that are filed to keep up with the quota demand in Brooklyn.[111] He was marked as a troublemaker. A supervisor told him: "The mayor's looking for it, the police commissioner's looking for it … every commanding officer wants to show it." Get with the program. Schoolcraft has it on tape.

Shortly thereafter Schoolcraft became ill at work and went home. A dozen police supervisors came to his house, told the landlord he was suicidal, and got the key to his apartment. They dragged him away in handcuffs and seized his tape recorder and papers. By lying to the hospital authorities, they forced him into a Queens mental ward for six days. But they missed the backup tape recorder in his apartment.

Schoolcraft gave his tapes to the *Village Voice*. In a turnabout similar to the P.S. 33 test scores, when the Schoolcraft case became public, the 81st Precinct could no longer fake the numbers; felony assaults jumped 76 percent. Ray Kelly is investigating.

—◄○►—

John Eterno, a former police captain who now chairs the Department of Criminal Justice at Molloy College, and Eli Silverman, a professor at John Jay College of Criminal Justice, published a survey in 2010 of retired NYPD supervisors, more than a hundred of whom said that intense pressure to show a decline in crime had led to manipulation of statistics.

Mike and the NYPD attacked the report. Eterno pointed to Schoolcraft's tape recordings:

These tapes are an independent source of data that supports just about everything we found. You're seeing relentless pressure, questionable activities, and unethical manipulation of statistics. We've lost the understanding that policing is not just about crime numbers, it's about service.

The NYPD isn't a police force out of control. It's a police force following the orders of an out-of-control mayor.

CHAPTER FOUR

The Final Outrage—
Maybe

—◦—

New Yorkers assumed Mike would be gone in 2009. By landslide margins, voters had twice established a two-term limit for the city's elected officials, first in a 1993 referendum, and again in 1996 when the city council placed yet another referendum on the ballot trying to extend its own term to 12 years. Mike always has had his eyes on Washington. He thought he'd be moving on after his second term. So in 2005, when the council was making noises about extending their own terms, here's what Mike had to say:[112]

"While it may be that the City Council has a right to override them, deliberately saying to the public, 'We don't care what you think,' I would use the word 'disgraceful'. The cynicism that that would engender towards city government is not something that this city needs. The public wants term limits, and if that's what they want, we should all learn to live with 'em."

As his second term was winding down and a place on the national ticket didn't pan out, Mike decided he wasn't leaving, no matter what the voters had decided.

As part of an orchestrated public relations campaign, thirty of New York's richest people published a letter urging the city council to override term limits so that Mike could run again.[113] The council didn't need convincing.

The Sturm und Drang that accompanied the final 29–22 Council vote was just Polibiz. The script had already been written; the ending was never in doubt. If they passed it, Mike would sign the bill. That's all they needed to know.

The *New York Times*, which had once said "We are wary of changing the rules just to suit the ambition of a particular politician," applauded the voter smackdown. Without irony, its endorsement said, "Term limits unfairly limit voters' choices." If publishing the *Pentagon Papers* marked a high point in the paper's 160-year history, its support of Mike's brazen third term taking will be remembered as one of the lowest.

The real estate lobby was delighted. Non-profit organizations that had received Mike's money and wanted more applauded the action or didn't dare criticize. His operatives called on some of them to testify at the legally mandated public hearing. They complied. In a time of fiscal crisis, they said, Mike was indispensable.[114] Who could say that with a straight face about the city council? But extending its term too was part of the deal. They used the word "continuity" and let it go at that.

On the day Mike announced his intention to sign the legislation, Al Sharpton's National Action Network received $50,000 from the Sharpton–Klein EEP.

Sharpton told the *New York Times*, "I'm leaning toward those who advocate in favor of making changes in the law through a referendum. But I haven't come to any final determination yet." A few days later, another $60,000 from EEP came in over the transom. Sharpton stopped leaning and said no more about term limits. Later, Sharpton would later say that he never got any of Mike's money: "not that I know of."[115]

A legally mandated hearing was held in the smallest room that could be found. With the conscience of a Wall Street investment banker marinated in the cynicism of New York's political culture, Mike sat stone-faced as New Yorkers stepped to the microphone and vented their anger to no avail. He would hold on to his office and the council members would keep theirs.

Council Speaker Christine Quinn had planned to run for mayor following Mike's second term. But she was embroiled in a slush-fund scandal still fresh in voters' minds. Buried in the budgets that Mike had negotiated with her were millions of dollars that had flowed not only to unworthy projects—a commonplace—but to non-existent entities! Few were watching when these fictional organizations vanished from the city's ledgers and the money flowed to her political allies. But some folks did notice. She retained a top criminal-defense lawyer. Mike wanted the scandal to go away too. A couple of low-level operatives were indicted, the city's Department of Investigation went to sleep, and the odd couple entered into a political marriage, a grotesque sight for anyone who had eyes to see and could bear to watch.[116]

New Yorkers didn't know much about the bride, but they were rip-roaring mad at the groom. Would they be as angry in November as they were in June?

With the help of Ira Glasser, former ACLU national director, author-columnist Nat Hentoff, and several other angry New Yorkers, I organized a group called Fed Up New Yorkers. We set up a website and published a small newspaper, distributing 25,000 copies around Greenwich Village and Lower Manhattan. Not much firepower next to the *New York Times*/Bloomberg/Wall Street/Real Estate gang, but we felt we had to do something.

Mike was still promoting the notion that the dirty business of politics wasn't for him. But how could he leave us in the middle of a fiscal crisis? "Progress, not politics" was his campaign slogan.

The Race Card Redux

The 2009 election featured the customary massive free and paid media campaign; a weak, underfinanced opponent; and testimonials from rich New Yorkers as well as those who had been bought or bullied into supporting him.

Mike was running against Comptroller William Thompson, a black man. Ten days before the election, the *Times* published a large, front-page photo of Mike treating Colin Powell to a hot dog at a fast-food joint.

Rudy Giuliani, still sniffing out the possibilities of higher office, accompanied him to a Jewish Community Council breakfast in Borough Park, Brooklyn. Rudy told the ultra-Orthodox Jews in attendance, "I worry daily that the city might be turned back to the way it was before 1993. And you know exactly what I'm talking about." Of course they did. Mike chimed in that without the right political leadership, New York "could become another Detroit." Colin Powell didn't attend that meeting.

After breakfast with the Orthodox Jews, Rudy and Mike went over to a Columbus Day parade in Howard Beach, Queens, the community forever embedded in the city's history as the ethnic enclave where a gang of young thugs brutally beat three black men who didn't "belong" in the neighborhood, chasing one of them out onto a highway to his death.

The Borough Park and Howard Beach campaign stops were no less calculating than the opening of Ronald Reagan's 1980 presidential campaign in the Mississippi town where three civil-rights workers were murdered. Mike was sending a message.

Neither Rev. Calvin Butts nor Rev. Al Sharpton was at the Borough Park or Howard Beach events, but Butts supported Mike all the way. "What could I say to a man who was mayor, and was supportive of a lot of programs that are important to me?" It wasn't about the money. It was about … about …? Sharpton supported Thompson—quietly.

―◄o►―

Mike squeezed out a 4.4 percent victory in the lowest turnout for a mayoral election in New York history, with barely a quarter of the city's registered voters casting ballots.[117] Again, Manhattan voters gave him his largest margin, 41,186 votes. They were drawn from the most affluent areas—*New York Times* readers. Mike's campaign organization had established a multimillion-dollar computerized database that enabled him to target his supporters with great efficiency. Christine Quinn held on to her seat, surviving a strong primary challenge.[118]

Before the election Mike had wired $1.1 million to the Independence Party's "housekeeping" account. Unlike expenditures by his official campaign account, Bloomberg for Mayor 2009 Inc., the money was listed as a donation to the Independence Party and was paid out by a trust he had established. Payments to housekeeping accounts are exempt from campaign contribution limits and this one wouldn't be made public until after the election. Previously, Mike had said that all campaign expenditures would flow through his official account so that voters would know before the election just how he was spending his money.

Giving money to a housekeeping account is a well-established mechanism for circumventing campaign finance regulations. But there was something more sinister in play. The campaign plan called for "ballot security and poll watching."

A veteran Republican campaign specialist who had come from Pataki's political operation to work on the first two Bloomberg campaigns received most of the funds. He didn't spend it on ballot security and poll watching. Nonetheless, the Independence Party seemed content to take a small percentage of the money and write John Haggerty a check for the balance. When reporters discovered the donation, a full-blown scandal erupted. Haggerty was indicted for grand larceny. At the trial, the defense argued that once the mayor gave the money to the Independence Party, it no longer belonged to him. He was not a victim. The jury was divided and seemingly confused, but eventually it convicted the defendant on a lesser count of larceny.

The larger questions were obscured by the frenzy over the indictment and trial. What was a "ballot security" operation and why did Mike want one? And why didn't he want anyone to know about it? This is another of those "emperor has no clothes" stories. So-called ballot security operations are aimed at suppressing votes in precincts with large minority populations. Voters are warned, for example, that if they go to the polling places and have outstanding traffic tickets, they risk arrest. Time and again, when Republicans are caught employing ballot security tactics, they say that these are "rogue operations," carried out without orders from the top.

Mike and the Republican Party are old hands at this game. Rudy Giuliani, for example, had many off-duty cops posted at polling places in black and Hispanic neighborhoods in 1993, the second time he ran against David Dinkins. Anonymous posters were put up near polling sites warning voters that immigration officers were present to deport illegal aliens. A hostile atmosphere is created. Sure, you might be legal, have no tickets and nothing to worry about. But stay away if you don't want trouble.

In the 2005 election, Freddy Ferrer filed a complaint with the Justice Department, saying that Mike's plan to use off-duty correction officers to guard polls in the Bronx was "an organized effort of voter intimidation disguised as poll watching." Mike's people said that he had no interest in suppressing minority votes. The mayor, they said, is just "ensuring the integrity of the system."

Mike professed not to recall much of anything about the 2009 transaction and said he hardly knew Haggerty, although he had been with him and top mayoral aides many times over a nine-year period and had personally escorted him to meetings of New York Republican leaders whose consent he needed to get back on the Republican ballot after he had left the party. As for the ballot security operations, in classic Bloomberg, he testified:

> *It's traditional, I'm told. The security is a process to make sure that people that want to vote have the right to vote and don't get pushed aside or denied the access to vote.*[119]

Kenneth Gross, Mike's chief campaign finance lawyer, told investigative reporter Aram Roston, "It is perfectly legal for the mayor to make a personal contribution to the Independence Party. We've done everything in compliance with applicable state and city law."

Cyrus Vance, the recently elected Manhattan DA, also talked about "the integrity of the electoral process." Roston quoted a former prosecutor who echoed the sentiments of many political observers as well as many of the jurors who thought Haggerty was a fall guy: "I was shocked that Cy Vance gave the mayor such a free ride. It seems that Vance has decided he doesn't have the stomach for it." But the million-dollar donation with its overtones of suppressing minority votes in a campaign against an opponent who was black was routine compared to the scandal that received virtually no attention. Even I was stunned.

Mike and His Opponent's Wife

Here is an excerpt from Wayne Barrett's January 2010 *Village Voice* cover story:

> *The mayor has directed or triggered between $43 million and $51 million in public and personal subsidies into a museum project led by Thompson's current wife and long-time companion, Elsie McCabe-Thompson, dumping $2 million of additional city funding into it as late as September 30, in the middle of the mayoral campaign. ... The museum ... is little more than an office in a warehouse in Long Island City, with no permanent art collection of its own, no gallery, no accreditation from*

the American Association of Museums or the Association of African American Museums, and no connection or history with Harlem ...[120]

Most people don't know the story. Some to whom I've mentioned it shrug it off. I try to explain. Say you've bet on the Yankees to win the American League pennant. They lose to the Boston Red Sox. Later it's discovered that the Red Sox owner paid the Yankee pitcher's wife tens of millions of dollars for some dinky warehouse space. Think there'd be a scandal that would reverberate for the next century, maybe even put some folks in jail? Maybe in sports, which most people believe are honestly competitive—as do I—but not in politics, not in New York, not now. Anyway, the *New York Times* must have missed that scandal.

CHAPTER FIVE

Mike,
Wall Street's Mayor

◄O►

Enron and other corporate scandals had begun to fade from public consciousness. Wall Street was booming. The bankers thought the time was ripe to push for even further deregulation. Bloomberg threw his weight behind it. The rationale was a familiar one: If New York City was to maintain its competitive position as a global financial center, it should not be hamstrung by regulation from Washington. In other words, don't let the government get between your banker and your life savings.

Many analysts had warned of the impending crash well before 2007 or even 2006. The FBI had warned about massive fraud in the mortgage markets as early as 2005. Mike dismissed them all. Right up to the collapse of Lehman Brothers, he was calling for less regulation, tight restrictions on punitive damages for defrauded investors, fewer capital requirements, and, in general, an even freer hand for Wall Street. He called it "reform."[121]

In January 2007, along with Sen. Chuck Schumer, whose political career is underwritten by Wall Street, Mike released a consultant's report that confirmed his view that Wall Street regulation was "devastating for both our city and our nation."[122]

After the collapse of Lehman Brothers and the ensuing financial collapse, reporters asked whether he had any comments on the new financial regulations that were being considered in Washington. He said, "No, I haven't looked at that. You know, I'll leave that to those people that are doing that full-time. I've got to worry about the city."

On April 30, 2010, he had safely returned to his City Hall bullpen, Wall Street had been bailed out, and he was ready to comment. He sat down for a televised chat with Larry Summers, hosted by Charlie Rose. Still pitching his luxury city vision, Mike said, "We've become the glitzy, the edgy, the where-it's-happening city around the world, and so our tourism business is down only two or three percent."

Then the inevitable question: What about the Great Wall Street debacle?

Said Mike: "There were a few investment banks that had overextended, had speculated beyond what was appropriate, and the bondholders and the shareholders got wiped out, which is appropriate. And the public didn't lose any money." Ho hum: The public didn't lose any money!

Summers, himself a hedge fund consultant and key enabler of the Great Wall Street Swindle, was now working for the Obama administration. He reminded Mike that millions of people lost their jobs and homes.

But Mike wasn't buying it. Greedy homeowners, Congress, Fannie and Freddie, the Community Reinvestment Act, etc. Let's not play the blame game. With money and persistence, Mike and the Boys may get away with the revisionist history. That they are determined to do so is clear.

Here he is on a November 1, 2011 panel with David Dinkins and Ed Koch.

It was not the banks that created the mortgage crisis. ... It was, plain and simple, Congress who forced everybody to go and to give mortgages to people who were on the cusp [and who] pushed Fannie and Freddie to make a bunch of loans that were imprudent; they were the ones that pushed the banks to loan to everybody.

But let's not focus on why we got here and who did it. It's fun to blame people and look to the past but it doesn't do anything for the future.

Even Koch, a Fan of Mike, couldn't let that one go. He noted the multimillion-dollar fines that the SEC levied against Goldman Sachs and Citigroup, and challenged Mike's story line:

What do you think they got fined for—schmutz on the sidewalk? They got fined because they abused their relationship with their clientele. And I want to see somebody—I want to see one of them, of a major corporation, punished criminally. They beggared the people in this country. More than $2 trillion was lost in the great recession.

Just one? Still, Mike must have been taken aback to hear those words from Koch. He was far more comfortable with Goldman Sachs executive Brian Griffiths who, in defending the post-collapse Wall Street bonuses, said: "The injunction of Jesus to love others as ourselves is a recognition of self-interest. ... We have to tolerate the inequality as a way to achieving greater prosperity and opportunity for all." And with Goldman CEO Lloyd Blankfein, who famously said that Goldman was "doing God's work."

Rolling Stone reporter and author Matt Taibbi has been tracking Wall Street's financial predations for years, understands the scams better than most, and makes them accessible to the uninitiated—I include myself in that very large universe. Mike's remarks got his attention. Taibbi's reaction is worth repeating at length.

> *He is a billionaire Wall Street creature with an extreme deregulatory bent who has quietly advanced some nastily regressive police policies (most notably the notorious "stop-and-frisk" practice) but has won over upper-middle-class liberals with his stances on choice and gay marriage and other social issues. ... He understands that as long as you keep muggers and pimps out of the prime shopping areas in the Upper West Side, and make sure to sound the right notes on abortion, stem-cell research, global warming, and the like, you can believably play the role of the wisecrack-ing, good-guy-billionaire Belle of the Ball for the same crowd that twenty years ago would have been feting Ed Koch.*

Whether the city returns to its old corrupt arrangements between real estate barons and politicians, or whether Mike is the canary in the coal mine for a post-Bloomberg permanent oligarchy remains to be seen, but either way, optimism is hard to sum-mon up.

Regarding Mike's condescending comments on the Occupy Wall Street protest-ers (it's okay to "sow some wild oats" but it's time to get back to work), Matt Taibbi said:

> *To me, this is Michael Bloomberg's Marie Antoinette moment, his own personal "Let Them Eat Cake" line. This one series of comments allows us to see under his would-be hip centrist Halloween mask and look closely at the corrupt, arrogant aristocrat underneath. ... This whole notion that the financial crisis was caused by government attempts to create an "ownership society" and make mortgages more available to low-income (and particularly minority) borrowers has been pushed for some time by dingbats like Rush Limbaugh and Sean Hannity ... nobody who actually understands anything about banking, or has spent more than ten min-utes inside a Wall Street office, believes any of that crap.*

Taibbi goes on to provide a short, riveting explanation of the Big Wall Street Swindle (read his latest book, *Griftopia*; it's all you have to know), and then in his classic nuanced style, he writes,

Well, you know what, Mike Bloomberg? FUCK YOU. People are not protesting for their own entertainment, you asshole. They're protesting because millions of people were robbed, by your best friends incidentally, and they want their money back.

Amen, Matt Taibbi. Wall Street, a culture so deeply corrupt and powerful, has brought about the current era of gangster capitalism. And Mike has at long last been outed as the Capo di tutti who sits in City Hall.

In light of Mike's $1-a-year salary, some may find that judgment too harsh. I'll end the story of Wall Street's Mayor with what I hope will contribute to the further unraveling of the image of the selfless public servant.

Bloomberg's ROI on His Investment in Politics

On January 18, 2012, a *New York Times* story appeared with this headline: "Bloomberg Says He Pays Highest Tax Rate and Opposes Hedge Fund Break":

When you take out the money I give to charity, then I pay the highest personal income tax rate," he said. "I don't even have carried interest or any of those things. I don't even have a lot of capital gains. It's virtually none. It is all the income from the company and it's taxable as ordinary income, and I pay the highest rate, state, city and federal.

The paper noted the secrecy surrounding his returns. We have to take him at his word. Nonetheless, the casual reader would have come away with the impression that Mike was a Warren Buffett kind of guy, even a candidate for the Occupy movement:

The mayor's statements echo the remarks of another billionaire, Warren E. Buffett, who is also an opponent of the carried interest exception. But they also pit Mr. Bloomberg against many Wall Street financiers who have fought to retain the lower tax rate.

The law doesn't require candidates to release their tax returns. Most candidates do. During election season, selected reporters are ushered into a guarded room to peek at sanitized versions of Mike's tax returns for two hours. No copying, no note taking, no dollar amounts.

Bloomberg LP is a private company. As such, it escapes much regulatory scrutiny. A team of forensic accountants armed with subpoenas couldn't track down how he grew his fortune from an estimated $1.3 billion in 1997, when he began thinking about politics, to perhaps $20 billion today. But thanks to some fine investigative reporting, we do know some things.

Bloomberg's Offshore Accounts

The Bloomberg Family Foundation sends hundreds of millions of dollars to offshore accounts in places like the Cayman Islands, Cyprus, Bermuda, and elsewhere.[123] The money then moves into hedge funds and other investments around the world. It's a tax dodge to avoid paying federal and New York taxes on what is called "unrelated business income." Former Manhattan District Attorney Robert Morgenthau tried to stop it, but couldn't. It's legal.

Mike isn't the only tax schemer, of course, but he's one of the heavyweights and nobody can come up with such mind-bending rationales. When the scheme was exposed, he said, "The less tax I pay, the more money I can put into charity."

Think how much better off we'd be if Mike and all those other billionaire philanthropists who use offshore accounts paid no taxes at all. The government could come to them directly and apply for grants and loans to finance schools, build bridges, pay social security benefits, and so on.

—◄o►—

Steven Rattner, a former *New York Times* reporter who left the paper to run a private equity firm, is Mike's investment adviser. He chaired Democrats for Bloomberg in 2005. Rattner has reported his net worth at between $188 and $608 million. In 2010, the Securities and Exchange Commission charged him with paying more than $1 million to former state comptroller Alan Hevesi's top political adviser. Rattner wanted the state pension fund to increase its investment in his private equity firm, the Quadrangle Group, from $100 million to $150 million. Rattner, according to the SEC, agreed to pay $6.2 million to settle the charges and agreed not to associate with any investment advisers or broker-dealers for two years.

Quadrangle paid $12 million to settle both the federal and state charges, and agreed to cooperate with the investigation by New York State Attorney General Andrew Cuomo. The firm severed its ties with Rattner, and said that what he had done was "inappropriate, wrong, and unethical." Maybe the lawyers cautioned them against using the word "illegal."

In November 2010, just after Cuomo was elected governor and before he took office, he filed lawsuits for $26 million against Rattner. On December 30, Rattner settled the case for $10 million, and was barred from appearing in any capacity before a public pension fund for five years. His PR guy said that he "shares with the New York Attorney General the goal of eliminating public pension-fund practices that are not in the public interest." Mike supported Cuomo for governor. Hevesi and his bagman went to jail.

Mike threw a book party for Rattner in the Grill Room of the Four Seasons. Arthur Sulzberger, Jr., the *New York Times* publisher, co-hosted it. Reportedly, Rattner is his financial adviser as well.

The city's Übermenschen turned out to honor one of their own. There was Robert Rubin, Jamie Dimon of J.P. Morgan Chase, Lloyd C. Blankfein of Goldman Sachs, Henry Kravis of Kohlberg Kravis, Tony James of the Blackstone Group, Vernon Jordan of Akin Gump, Roger Altman of Evercore, Alan Schwartz, formerly of Bear Stearns, and dozens of others, including Joel Klein, then chancellor of the city's public schools.

Bloomberg TV and the Comcast/NBC Universal Merger

In July 2010, a group calling itself the Coalition for Competition in Media sought to stop the merger of Comcast, the giant cable and internet vompany, and NBC Universal, the TV network. In a letter to two congressional subcommittee chairs, the group identified itself as "a coalition of public interest organizations, unions, small and minority media companies and independent programmers." The Coalition argued the proposed merger was "fundamentally threatening to the public interest."

Financed by the Nation Institute's Investigative Fund, Aram Roston dug into the real story of the Coalition, which was set up to look like a grassroots organization. Roston learned that it was "conceived, financed, and staffed by lobbyists for New York City Mayor Michael Bloomberg's $7 billion-per-year media company."

Bloomberg LP earns the bulk of its revenues from $20,000-a-year terminal leases, but it is aggressively expanding into journalism. The terminal revenues subsidize Bloomberg Television, a cable station.

In what appeared on the surface to be an effort to block the Comcast merger, Bloomberg hired a slew of Washington lobbyists, lawyers, and former Obama public relations staffers. Deputy Mayor Howard Wolfson's old firm, the Glover Park Group, a lobbying operation made up mostly of former Clinton people, organized the "grassroots" effort.

Unlike the other Coalition members, Bloomberg's main goal was not to block the merger, but to pressure Comcast to place Bloomberg TV next to CNBC, a concept known as "neighborhooding," whereby channels that offer similar coverage are placed close to one another so that viewers can discover them more easily.

Lisa Graves, director of the Center for Media and Democracy, told Roston that "[The Coalition] is like a front group because the name of the group and the superficial appearance obscure the primary intent, which is to further the company's corporate interest."

During the antimerger campaign, *Bloomberg BusinessWeek* published the story that Comcast's political action committee had more than doubled its donations to politicians to $1.1 million. Glover Park reproduced the story and sent it around to reporters. A Bloomberg spokeswoman assured the press there is "an impenetrable firewall" between editorial decisions and the other parts of the company.

The FCC approved the merger, but conditioned its approval on Comcast's agreement to "neighborhood" channels. The Coalition's public interest groups viewed the decision as a major defeat for the viewing public. One group called it "a devastating loss."

Bloomberg LP president Dan Doctoroff uncorked the champagne. He put out a celebratory press release: "The FCC has taken strong action to preserve independent news programming, and protect competitors against discrimination."

Bloomberg TV and Time Warner

Funny thing about the Yankees on your Time Warner cable box. A few years ago, the Yanks were in a murderers' row with several other sports channels. Mets games are broadcast on SNY at 26. MSG, the Madison Square Garden Channel, owns 27. Sports heavyweights ESPN and ESPN2 have 28 and 29.[124]

That's an excerpt from Wayne Barrett's story on the relationship between Bloomberg TV and TimeWarner.

In March 2008, Time Warner, whose lucrative ten-year contract with the city was about to expire, moved Bloomberg Television from Channel 104 into the Yankees spot. The Yankees had been broadcasting its games on Channel 30 ("Yes" network). Now they would be broadcast on Channel 53, after the Learning Channel. It was the flip side of the Comcast campaign. Bloomberg TV has nothing to do with sports. It was in the wrong neighborhood.

The smoking gun hasn't been found. Dan Doctoroff had overseen the city's cable franchises before he left City Hall to become president of Bloomberg LP. Two months after he took up his new post, Time Warner made the switch.

"You can be sure," Barrett wrote, "that Time Warner believes that its decision to bump the Yankees and move a minor news network all the way from channel 104 to a prime spot on the dial carries some weight with the city and the man who runs it." Michael Bloomberg denies any personal involvement in the discussions over the license renewal.

There were the predictable denials, the limited hangouts, and the stonewalling from other players in the story. "Meanwhile," Barrett pointed out, "in the rest of the country, Bloomberg TV remains in the cable hinterlands: It's still at 224 in Los Angeles, 252 in San Diego, 246 in Boston, and, like it once was in New York, 104 in New Jersey. (Cablevision, which has the city contract in the Bronx and parts of Brooklyn, has Bloomberg TV at 105.)"

Bloomberg Terminal Customers and City Subsidies?

During the last mayoral campaign Mike was asked about his wealth. He said that Bloomberg LP isn't a publicly traded company so "I don't know what's happened to my wealth."

Even the *New York Times* said the answer was ridiculous; "strains credulity" was the polite phrase. "Mr. Bloomberg owns the vast majority of Bloomberg LP and is regularly briefed on its performance, which is a real-time barometer of his wealth. His investments in mutual funds and bonds are managed by outside advisers, but these people give him updates on their value. And he employs a small army of accountants, who keep close tabs on his finances."[125]

Michael White, in his "Noticing New York" blog, has been following Mike's political and business interests as closely as the opaque arrangements allow.[126] Wayne Barrett has raised similar conflict of interest questions regarding this next story.

White reports that when Mike first took office in 2002, he and his lawyers negotiated a ruling with the Conflict of Interests Board (COIB) in which he agreed to release a list of his company's 100 biggest customers. Only if a customer constituted 10 percent or more of Bloomberg LP's total sales would the Board consider it a potential conflict and require him "to seek further advice." He told the COIB that the largest customer on the list accounted for less than 4 percent of total revenue, or about a $250 million per year.

As White puts it, the practical effect of the ruling is that a customer who is doing more than half a billion dollars worth of business with Bloomberg LP can "still walk into the mayor's office to get a land use or contract approval without tripping an alarm." The rationale for the 10 percent rule is inexplicable. In any case, the COIB doesn't or can't verify Mike's compliance; his conflicts are more or less what he says they are.

White: "Bloomberg LP customers like Goldman Sachs, Bear Stearns, AIG, Citigroup, Credit Suisse, Deutsche Bank, HSBC Bank, J.P. Morgan Chase, Lehman Brothers, Bank of New York, Tullett & Tokyo, Morgan Stanley, GFI, State Street Bank, and Merrill Lynch have all hired lobbyists to lobby the Bloomberg administration, with several specifying the mayor's office. Of the 124 companies on the customer list, 33 appear on the Campaign Finance Board's list of companies doing business with the city. And that's just the Campaign Finance Board's list."

Barrett: "Goldman Sachs had so many issues before the administration that it took seven pages to list its lobbying activities in the city clerk system (it spent almost a million dollars). When the city and state approved $1.6 billion in low-cost, tax-exempt bonds for Goldman's new downtown headquarters in 2005, Doctoroff justified it by saying that Wall Street's top firm might otherwise leave the city. Goldman Sachs is moving to Kansas, right? The *Daily News* editorialized that Bloomberg was 'taken to the cleaners' in the Goldman deal. The city and state are in line to forfeit a whopping $321 million to Goldman because the governor and mayor agreed to contract terms that were downright foolhardy."

We don't know how much business Goldman did with Bloomberg LP before Mike became mayor or how much business it does today. The idea that the city was taken to the cleaners by Goldman Sachs and Bloomberg seems not to have occurred to the *News* editorial writers.

One thing is clear: Mike's claims of impregnable firewalls between his business, political, philanthropic, and government interests strain credulity.

Conclusion

Michael Bloomberg's plan for New York is a sanitized version of Roger Starr's Planned Shrinkage: luxury for the few, austerity for the many. He took over the machinery of government, paid off the city's civic, religious, and labor leaders, aligned himself with the richest New Yorkers, including especially the city's three major newspaper owners, and sought to make the city a "glitzy, happening place" to live and work for people who could afford it.

He leveraged the city's balance sheet and ate away at its already weak political institutions with brazen payoffs. He gave billions to firms like Goldman Sachs and to the city's real estate developers.

The taxpayer money he gave away will never be recouped in jobs created, small businesses saved, families protected. The neighborhoods he destroyed will never recover, and the lost opportunity to make the public schools better won't come around again for generations, if ever.[127] But maybe the most damaging legacy of all is the governance model he introduced: the mega-billionaire who slid easily between bullshitting the people when he could and telling them to go fuck themselves when he couldn't.

Nothing can excuse the overriding of term limits. But it's our shame as well as his. Too many would-be citizens have bought into the idea that politics doesn't matter. Here is Sir Bernard Crick on that subject:

> The person who wishes not to be troubled by politics and to be left alone finds himself the unwitting ally of those to whom politics is a troublesome obstacle to their well-meant intentions to leave nothing alone.
>
> All over the world, there are men aspiring to power and there are actual rulers who, however many different names they go by, have in common a rejection of politics.

As corrupt as our politics are, there is no alternative to politics. More informed citizens and less money is the answer to that corruption. The campaign slogan "progress, not politics" is an insidious idea. Mayors aren't CEOs and citizens aren't employees; New York City isn't a luxury product and we aren't customers.

In January 2014, Mike is supposed to be gone.

But we probably haven't heard the last of him.

Explanations and Acknowledgments

I have an embarrassingly large number of people to thank for such a short book so long in the making. Bloomberg had not yet completed his first term when I began writing an account of our fight at Independence Plaza and his role in it. Immodestly, I suppose, I thought it was worth sharing the experience of organizing tenants against the real estate lobby, the politicians and the housing bureaucrats who, under Bloomberg, continue to privatize and deregulate as much of the city's rent-regulated housing stock as quietly as they can.

At the risk of being labeled a crank, I also wanted to caution against tenant advocates who presented themselves as insiders. I never met one who was. Many were sincere but ignorant or, more politely, were knowledgeable about the wrong things. For example, tenants typically retained lawyers who knew everything there was to know about the laws and regulations surrounding the Mitchell-Lama program. They also knew how to litigate. So they brought lawsuits based on the Mitchell-Lama laws and regulations. But the insiders long ago had rigged these laws in favor of the real estate operators. I couldn't help thinking of these tenant lawyers as idiot savants.[128] The tenants usually ran out of money to sustain the lawsuits and were forced into disastrous settlements. Politics almost always trumps law. That unfailing truth and an understanding of the terms of trade between the politicians who make the laws and the insiders who finance their campaigns sometimes were hard truths to sell to tenants who, along with most people, don't trust politicians in the abstract but often are taken in by those who claim to represent them.

A book on New York politics and real estate was a hard sell too. Commercial publishers aren't interested in books that seem destined for the remainder bins at Strand Books. Still, it was the book I wanted to write. So I wrote it. A very good literary agent helped me with a proposal. He submitted it to NYU Press. A few weeks later he reported that the proposal had been rejected. They didn't want to see the manuscript. The message was, "We don't do memoirs."

I thought that was bizarre. But the prospect of query letters to publishers, revised proposals, rejections, and so on was an unappealing way to spend the next few years. I shelved the manuscript and got on with my life. When Bloomberg overrode term limits I took it off the shelf. That brazen "fuck you" to New York voters and his Hamptons on the Hudson vision fit nicely into the real estate and politics story I wanted to tell. If that story was to be labeled a memoir, it would be his, not mine.

As my direct experience with him was limited to the Independence Plaza story, I wrote what I envisioned as conversations he might have had with his political advisors on a much broader range of subjects. These imaginary dialogues were informed by my own experience in New York politics and government. I've been in those rooms and through those conversations learned how things work from the inside. But I didn't have the writing chops to pull off what essentially was a play. The dialogue was stilted, uninteresting.

Meg Knox, a freelance editor from Boulder Colorado, took an axe to the unwieldy dialogue and reshaped it into narrative form. So thank you Meg Knox for taking that painful, necessary first step. Many other folks contributed to getting the book into its present shape. Bill Fares, John Morrow, Terry Reed, Jessie Singer, Dan Browne, and others worked on various aspects of the book; so many others that I can't remember them all—and won't try. I would fail to mention some people and they would be justifiably upset. I apologize for that. Then again, many of them may be grateful. Matt Hall, a New York real estate lawyer, had nothing to do with the book but he helped me set up the tenant organization at Independence Plaza and I'm not sure I ever thanked him for it. So thanks, Matt. Finally, there were so many tenants at Independence Plaza who did such great work that were I to name them all this acknowledgment would go on for pages. I thank those who still talk to me.

My deepest thanks go to the investigative reporters, scholars, and public interest groups who were on to Bloomberg soon after he took office and who reported what they had discovered. I've used their work together with his public statements—the spin versus the facts—to paint what I think is an accurate picture of the character and meaning of Wall Street's Mayor and his supporters. The endnotes reference the many sources I've drawn from. It isn't enough credit, but as a reader, I know extended acknowledgments are boring. This one is already longer than I intended. But I do want to single out three investigative journalists for special thanks, not in the usual way that a writer thanks the people who have read and commented on a draft—I was not in a position to ask—but as a New Yorker. For decades, they have been turning over the rocks to reveal the slithering mass of corruption and greed that is and always has been New York/Wall Street politics. It has taken on a new and more venal aspect under this mayor. In different ways, each of them has recognized Bloomberg's unique role.

Juan Gonzalez, *Daily News* columnist since 1987 and co-host of *Democracy Now!*, has written about the Bloomberg-led class war with its ethnic and racial subtexts. His analyses of the mechanisms by which Bloomberg has—perhaps successfully—locked in the rule of the bankers and real estate barons long after he's gone is the best I've read.[129]

◄o►

It's a testament to the single-minded ambition and callousness of New York politicians that they can show themselves in public, let alone stand for reelection, after Wayne Barrett has finished with them. Column after column for forty years, nobody has come close to the body of work that Barrett has produced. In his own words, "The greatest prize I've ever won for the work I've done in these pages was when Al D'Amato called me a 'viper' in his memoir."

Barrett's cover story in the *Village Voice* on the tens of millions of dollars that Bloomberg gave in public and private funds before and during the 2009 mayoral election to the dubious museum project run by his opponent's wife, and the *Times'* failure to report that scandal, are powerful proofs, if any more are needed, that Wall Street's Mayor and the paper of record are comrades in arms on the front lines of the increasingly obvious class war.[130] Its support for Bloomberg and what he represents extends far beyond its editorial page endorsements of his re-elections. The *Times* has been indispensable both in carrying forward Bloomberg's false narrative and in establishing a bogus history of his regime. It began with Bill Keller, the paper's op-ed editor when Bloomberg first ran for office. Keller became the executive editor at the beginning of Bloomberg's first term and remained in that post well into his third.

◄○►

Chris Hedges, a fifteen-year *Times* foreign correspondent, understands the paper's culture from the inside. In critiquing a documentary film, *Page One: Inside the* New York Times, Hedges said this:

> *The film should have looked more carefully at the colorless editor of the paper, Bill Keller ... a vocal cheerleader for the war in Iraq ... Keller, whose on-camera comments are bland and vapid, represents the ascendancy of neocons inside as well as outside* The New York Times. *... Senior editors such as Keller and Tanenhaus (book editor) are products of the time. They do not question the utopian faith in globalization. They support preemptive war, at least before it goes horribly wrong. And they accept unfettered capitalism, despite what it has done to the nation, as a kind of natural law. ... The inability to see that major centers of corporate power are criminal enterprises that are plundering the nation and destroying the ecosystem is evidence not of objectivity but moral bankruptcy.*
>
> *The lifestyle sections of the paper are rife with stories about fancy restaurants in New York, summer happenings in the Hamptons, designer*

wardrobes, expensive cars, exotic vacations, and exclusive private schools that are accessible to only a tiny percentage of rich Americans. The headline in Sunday's Real Estate section is typical: "It's July. Do You Know Where Your Beach House Is?"[131]

So thank you Chris Hedges, Wayne Barrett, Juan Gonzalez, Bob Herbert, Aram Roston, Graham Rayman, Tom Robbins, Matt Taibbi, and thank you to the Nation Institute, The New York Civil Liberties Union, the Fiscal Policy Institute, and yes, even the Manhattan Institute whose views on all things political are diametrically opposed to mine, but whose scholars, or at least some of them, share my revulsion for this Mayor. And finally, thank you Adrian Schoolcraft, the rookie cop who objected to the wholesale police abuses he had witnessed—and was forced to go along with—until he refused. He was promptly whisked away to a psychiatric ward. Schoolcraft is my nominee for a Frank Serpico Medal of Honor, yet to be established. This city needs one.

Endnotes

1. "Mayor Says New York Is Worth the Cost," *The New York Times*, Jan. 3, 2003, p. B3.
2. Jason L. Riley, a member of the *Wall Street Journal*'s editorial board, observed in an October 16, 2008 column that "instead of using the flush-year surpluses (due to booming Wall Street profits) to put New York's fiscal house in order, Mr. Bloomberg mostly squandered them."
3. See the Citizens Budget Commission report, Sep. 13, 2011, http://www.cbcny.org/print/1434.
4. To understand just how extreme the disparity of wealth and income has become during the Bloomberg era, consider a few salient facts from a landmark study carried out by the Fiscal Policy Institute, a well-respected New York progressive policy research institute. Following the 2001–03 recession, the income share of the top 1 percent of New Yorkers saw its fastest growth in 30 years, climbing to 44 percent in 2007. The top 1 percent in New York City has an income share almost twice that of the 23.5 percent historically high national level. The wealthiest 5 percent of the city's population had 58 percent of total income in 2007. In the middle of the 2002–07 expansion, the income share of New York City's top 1 percent passed that of the "middle" 45 percent. While the income of the average New York City household in the bottom 95 percent declined slightly, the average income among the city's top 5 percent increased by 85 percent. And among the richest 1 percent of New York City households, average real income more than doubled. http://www.fiscalpolicy.org/FPI_GrowTogetherOrPullFurtherApart_20101213.pdf.
5. "Making the Rent, 2002 to 2005: Changing Rent Burdens & Housing Hardships among Low-Income New Yorkers," December 2006, The Community Service Society.
6. "Reviving the City of Aspiration," Center for an Urban Future, September, 2009: www.nycfuture.org/CityOfAspiration.pdf.
7. *On Bullshit*, Princeton University Press, 2005.
8. William Andrews Clark, according to his son. Quoted in *The Battle for Butte: Mining and Politics on the Northern Frontier, 1864–1906*, Michael P. Malone and William L. Lang, University of Washington Press, 2006.
9. *Mike Bloomberg: Money, Power, Politics*, Joyce Purnick, Public Affairs, 2009.
10. *Liar's Poker*, Michael Lewis, Penguin, 1990, p. 213.
11. *Liar's Poker*, p. 52.

12. *Bloomberg by Bloomberg*, Michael R. Bloomberg, John Wiley & Sons, 2001, p. 25.

13. *Liar's Poker*, p. 198.

14. *Bloomberg by Bloomberg*.

15. As cited in *13 Bankers: The Wall Street Takeover and The Next Financial Meltdown*, Simon Johnson and James Kwak, First Vintage Books, 2011, p. 92 fn 11.

16. Sexual harassment claims surfaced in his first campaign but never got much traction. Now they are yesterday's news. See "Shut Your Mouth: Big-Bucks Bloomy Buys Corporate Silence in Six Sex and Race Cases," *Village Voice*, 2005-10-25; http://www.zimbio.com/Mayor+Michael+Bloomberg/articles/9/ Mayor+Michael+Bloomberg+Jekyll+Hyde+Redux; "Sex Suit Could Be A Problem for Bloomberg," http://www.huffingtonpost.com/huff-wires/20070729/ bloomberg-sexual-harassment/.

17. "Bloomberg's Surge: His Path to Power on Three Big Stages," Greg Sargent, *The New York Observer*, December 23, 2001.

18. "The Mayor and His Money," http://nymag.com/nymetro/news/people/ features/14573/.

19. "With More Private Giving Bloomberg Forges Ties," Sam Roberts and Jim Rutenberg, *New York Times*, May 23, 2005.

20. "Time for a Gut Rehab," Pratt Center for Community Development, June 2006.

21. www.counterpunch.org/2006/08/21/mayor-bloomberg-goes-to-quot-post-cath- olic-quot-ireland.

22. "The Bloomberg Machine," *Business Week*, April 23, 2001.

23. A month after the election, he went back with Rudy Giuliani and put a paper prayer to God into a crack in the Wailing Wall. He went again August 2003. This time he wore a red, white, and blue skullcap, and kissed the Wailing Wall. In 2005, he went again. During the 2008 presidential campaign, Mike criticized the spurious campaign tactics that promoted the notion that Obama had Muslim loyalties and thus might undermine America's support for Israel. He said, "Israel is just being used as a pawn, which is not that surprising, since some people are willing to stoop to any level to win an election." http://cityroom.blogs.nytimes. com/2008/06/20/bloomberg-criticizes-whisper-campaign-around-obama/.

24. Sources on Newman, Fulani, the Independence Party, and the *New York Times* treatment of the group and Bloomberg's involvement with it include "Psychopolitics: Inside the Independence Party of Fred Newman," Rita Nissan, www.ny1.com/?ArID=77825; "In New York, Fringe Politics in Mainstream," Michael Slackman, *New York Times*, May 28, 2005, http://www.nytimes. com/2005/05/28/nyregion/28party; "What the New York Times and Mayor

Bloomberg Don't Want You to Know about the Newman-Fulani Cult," www. lyndonlarouchewatch.org/nyt.htm; "Bloomberg's Therapist: Mayor Mike's Independence Party Friends Can Put Him on the Couch," www.villagevoice. com/2005-06-14/news/bloomberg-s-therapist/.

25. The *Village Voice*'s Tom Robbins has reported in depth on the Staten Island mob, its political connections, and the Bloomberg–Molinaro mutually supportive relationship: www.villagevoice.com/2005-10-11/news/the-odd-couple/; www.villagevoice.com/2002-06-18/news/island-in-the-schemes/.

26. See http://www.nlpc.org/stories/2005/12/05/staten-island-politician-does-odd-deals, a report of the National and Legal Policy Center.

27. See "Beep's close ties to mafia-linked builder," Greg B. Smith, Sunday, October 23, 2005. http://articles.nydailynews.com/2005-10-23/news/18317704_1_ciccone-guy-molinari-warehouse.

28. Ray Harding, former Liberal Party chief, who had given the ballot line to Giuliani in both mayoral campaigns, set up a real estate law and lobbying firm with Badillo. The two men lobbied the Giuliani administration for real estate developers. Harding's two sons and some Liberal Party stalwarts were given high positions in city government. Harding later pled guilty to a felony securities fraud charge in connection with the state comptroller pension fund scandal. http://articles.nydailynews.com/2011-05-17/news/29569999_1_ray-harding-hank-morris-pension-fund.

29. During a 2011 radio interview on the Brian Lehrer show, Joyce Purnick, who had written a friendly biography of Mike, extolled his handling of the sexual harassment charges, citing Mike's full disclosures. She contrasted his forthright approach with Herman Cain's stonewalling.

30. Some of Green's staffers had attended the meeting in which the anti-Sharpton literature was discussed. Reportedly, they had opposed it but hadn't walked out. Green was criticized for not firing anyone.

31. "In America; Democrats Make Nice (Finally)," http://www.nytimes. com/2001/10/22/opinion/in-america-democrats-make-nice-finally.

32. "Mike in Religion Pitch," Michael R. Blood, *Daily News*, August 17, 2001.

33. "Correspondent, Up with Moguls! Exploit the Rich!" *New York Times*, November 3, 2001.

34. A "razzle" is carnival lingo for a game designed to deceive its players. With thanks to Charles Denson, a Coney Island native and historian, who applied the word to Mike's plan to gentrify Coney Island: http://cityroom.blogs.nytimes. com/2009/07/15/answers-about-the-preservation-of-coney-island/.

35. Cited in "More than Words? Bloomberg and Race," Jarrett Murphy, *City Limits*, October 19, 2009.

36. "Mayor Bloomberg: The Rev. Al Sharpton a 'calming influence on the city,'" Kathleen Lucadamo, *Daily News*, April 2, 2009.

37. "The Ecumenist, Russ Baker," *The American Prospect*, November 30, 2002.

38. http://www.nytimes.com/2005/01/03/nyregion/03endorse.

39. "Mayor Deprives Rival of Black Clergy's Support," http://www.nytimes.com/2009/10/29/nyregion/29ministers; "Powerful Harlem Church Is also a Powerful Harlem Developer," http://www.nytimes.com/2008/08/18/nyregion/18abyssinian.

40. The exact amounts are unknown, but Mike has given large sums to the All Stars Project since he became Mayor. "What's Up and Spans City? Bloomberg's Philanthropy," Thomas J. Lueck, *New York Times*, August 17, 2005.

41. Susan Fainstein, Professor of Urban Planning, *Harvard Design Magazine*, Spring/Summer 2005, No. 22.

42. The Pulitzer Prize–winning biography of Robert Moses, *The Power Broker* by Robert A. Caro (Vintage Books, 1975), is as relevant today under the rule of Bloomberg as it was when Caro wrote it. Before writing the book, Caro had been *Newsday*'s Albany bureau chief .

43. "CitizenBloomberg:HowOurMayorHasGivenUstheBusiness,"www.villagevoice.com/2011-07-20/news/michael-bloomberg-harry-siegel-citizen-bloomberg/2/.

44. Center for an Urban Future, www.nycfuture.org/images_pdfs/pdfs/CityOfAspiration.pdf.

45. Dr. Mark Naison of Fordham University, as cited in "More than Words? Bloomberg and Race," Jarrett Murphy, *City Limits*, October 19, 2009.

46. *Bloomberg's New York: Class and Governance in the Luxury City*, University of Georgia Press, 2011.

47. This is the only cartoon that isn't Keith Seidel's. It was drawn by R.J. Matson, the editorial cartoonist at the *St. Louis Post-Dispatch*, *The New York Observer*, and *Roll Call*. 48.   "Yankee Stadium and Citi Field Are the Houses That You Built," http://articles.nydailynews.com/2009-01-17/sports/17914104_1_yankee-deal-citi-field-tax-free-bonds.

48. The New York City Department of Housing and Preservation.

49. With special thanks to Lo Faber whose website furnished some of the details for this account.

50. "Albany's Travesty of Democracy," *City Journal*, Spring 1997

51. Trump testimony given to the 1988 New York State Commission on Government Integrity. In that same hearing, Ethan Geto also testified to his role as a bundler.

52. When Mike ran in 2009, he pressed hard to get it. He failed because the teachers union blocked it. As I write, Mike and the teachers union are at war.

53. In 2008, the Democrats took control of both houses of the legislature and the governor's office for the first time since 1935. They openly demanded and received larger contributions from the real estate lobby. No meaningful tenant bills were passed.

54. Out of my presence, Ethan got him to agree to spread the 10 percent over a three-year period

55. The tenants are now in a lawsuit. Following the settlement, a lawyer for another Mitchell-Lama development, which had reached agreement with its owner, discovered that the owner hadn't disclosed a statutory tax benefit that required the development to remain in rent stabilization. The housing agency allowed Gluck retroactively to repay the subsidies he had collected. A lower court reversed the regulatory decision, calling it a legal fiction.

56. "Deal Would Limit Increases in Rent at a Tribeca Complex," David Chen, *New York Times*, March 9, 2004.

57. *New York Times*, June 29, 2004.

58. "Extinction," Katrina Lencek-Inagaki from *The Suburbanization of New York*, Jerilou Hammett and Kingsley Hammett (eds), Princeton Architectural Press, 2007, pp. 107–111.

59. The 1926 Limited Dividend Housing Companies Law, pioneered by New York Governor Al Smith, was based on bank financing. The Mitchell-Lama program gave the developers direct government financing and allowed for rentals as well as cooperatives.

60. Where bridge and tunnel tolls can be counted on to pay off the bondholders whose loans finance these public projects, the state can sell revenue bonds that carry low interest rates. For subsidized housing projects, however, revenues are less certain and bondholders want either general obligation bonds or higher interest rates.

61. *The Man Who Saved New York: Hugh Carey and the Great Fiscal Crisis of 1975*, Seymour P. Lachman and Robert Polner, State University of New York Press, 2010.

62. *The Cost of Good Intentions: New York City and the Liberal Experiment, 1960–1975*, Charles R. Morris, W.W. Norton, 1980, p. 185.

63. *The Rise and Fall of New York City*, Roger Starr, Basic Books, 1985, pp. 226–229. Ed Koch wrote the foreword.

64. As quoted in Charles Kaiser, "Blacks and Puerto Ricans, a Bronx Majority," *New York Times*, April 19, 1976, p. 23. See also Starr's defense, "Making New York Smaller," *New York Times*, Sunday Magazine, November 14, 1976. [Cited in *The Assassination of New York*, Robert Fitch, Verso Books, 1993.]

65. Report to the Governor by the New York State Moreland Act Commission on the Urban Development Corporation and Other State Financing Agencies,

"Restoring Credit and Confidence: A Reform Program for New York State and Its Public Authorities," March 31, 1976.

66. Few recall Koch's accommodation with Raymon Velez, the Bronx head of an antipoverty empire. Koch, as a campaigner, promised to dry up the public money flowing to "poverty pimps"; Koch, as mayor, gave Velez tens of millions in antipoverty funds and even a cable franchise.

67. Jack Newfield and Wayne Barrett described the meeting in *City for Sale: Ed Koch and the Betrayal of New York*, Harper & Row, 1988.

68. New York State Office of the Deputy State Comptroller for the City of New York, "NY City Planning Commission Granting Special Permits for Bonus Floor Area," Report A-23-83 (September 15, 1988), as cited in: *A Phoenix in the Ashes: The Rise and Fall of the Koch Coalition in New York City Politics*, John Hull Mollenkopf, 1992, Princeton University Press.

69. "Charges on Donations Made in Mayoral Race," Joyce Purnick, *New York Times*, August 15, 1985.

70. "The Empire and Ego of Donald Trump," Marylin Bender, *New York Times*, August 7, 1983.

71. "Leichter Says Builders Gave Most to Members of Board of Estimate," Josh Barnabel, *New York Times*, November 27, 1985.

72. "Big Donors to Top City Oficials Named," Frank Lynn, *New York Times*, December 23, 1986.

73. "No Posse Around Here," Russell Baker, *New York Times*, June 13, 1987.

74. You can go to this website and see all the plan's iterations: http://www.nyc.gov/html/hpd/html/about/plan.shtml.

75. Readers who would like to read a more balanced account of Mike's housing policies than I am able to offer might turn to *City Limits* magazine. See, for example, "Bloomberg Housing Plan Hits Milestones, Obstacles," Patrick Arden, http://www.citylimits.org/news/articles/4431/bloomberg-housing-plan-hits-milestones-obstacles.

76. A journalist, Norman Oder, has done great work reporting on all aspects of the Atlantic Yards real estate/politics boondoggle. Google "Atlantic Yards Report." See also "Develop Don't Destroy Brooklyn" at www.dddb.net.

77. Until 1989, when the US Supreme Court declared the Board of Estimate in violation of its one man–one vote rule, the Board had a substantial say over the city budget and land use. Each of the five borough presidents had one vote on the Board. The mayor, comptroller, and city council president each had two votes. Through a practice known as "borough courtesy," the borough presidents generally went along with the decision of the borough president in whose borough the project was proposed to be built. This meant that a

developer who wanted to build something in Brooklyn, for example, had to be on good terms with its borough president. That worthy was most likely to be a factotum controlled by the county leader. The elimination of the Board of Estimate and the devolution of much of its power to the mayor meant that City Hall would dominate the decisions on what was built in the city. Some of the land use powers exercised by the old Board of Estimate are now held by the city council. Developers who want to build in a council member's district are expected to take into account the member's feelings.

78. "Ratner Faces Atlantic Yards Hurdles," *Crain's New York*, November 8, 2009.

79. http://www.nypost.com/p/news/local/brooklyn/preacher_suite_deal_NR46iRQ dEPETlHp4jlI5mL#ixzz1ISQUCDch; http://atlanticyardsreport.blogspot.com/ 2011/04/post-focuses-on-daughtry.html.

80. A not-for-profit corporation that raises millions of dollars from real estate developers and other rich people who do business with the city. The Fund gives the money to causes deemed to be worthy. Patti Harris chairs the board. Mike appoints all the board members.

81. "Bloomberg's Do-Gooder Charity," Reid Pillifant, *New York Observer*, June 2, 2010.

82. *The Daily News* called his comments an "endorsement" of the sale. The *Times* later said that "the Bloomberg administration supported Tishman Speyer's record-breaking purchase."

83. "Bloomberg Flips on Stuy Town," Eliot Brown, *New York Observer*, January 8, 2010.

84. Wayne Barrett's extensive review of this and other conflicts can be found at www.villagevoice.com/content/printVersion/1338285/.

85. Vallone's chief of staff went on to head up the misleadingly named Rent Stabilization Association, a major landlord lobbying group whose mission is to eliminate rent stabilization.

86. "Neighborhood Report: Kips Bay; Tenants Battle for Low Rents, and a Diverse Building," Michael Gwertzman, *New York Times*, August 1, 2004.

87. One group of tenants sued to overturn the buyout. The state's highest court ruled that only the city had legal standing to raise the issue. It declined to do so.

88. http://www.mikebloomberg.com/index.cfm?objectid=4E5ABBA7-219B-8B95-7CE79D9EE12630E4.

89. See the report produced by the Coalition for the Homeless, Homeless Families at Risk, http://www.coalitionforthehomeless.org/pages/homeless-families-at-risk.

90. http://www.coalitionforthehomeless.org/blog/entry/ unhinged-from-reality-mayor-bloomberg-defends-his-shelter-denial-plan/.

91. In 2009, a collection of essays was published entitled *NYC Schools Under Bloomberg and Klein: What Parents, Teachers, and Policymakers Need to Know,* http://www.lulu.com/product/paperback/nyc-schools-under-bloomberg-klein-what-parents-teachers-and-policymakers-need-to-know/4970767. Liberals and conservatives, parents and teachers, scholars and activists contributed to the book. What they had in common was a deep understanding of how Mike and Joel covered their failed policies with bullshit and intimidation. This section draws heavily on their insights. Rather than lard it with references, I refer the reader to the original source. Along with everyone who cares about the city's schools, I'm indebted to the contributors but make no claim that they or any of them would agree with everything I've written here.

92. "Bloomberg, in Israel Trip, Shies away from Religiosity," Jim Rutenberg, *New York Times*, March 17, 2005.

93. http://www.nytimes.com/2007/11/16/education/16scores.

94. http://www.nytimes.com/2010/03/10/nyregion/10graduation.

95. http://www.city-journal.org/html/17_3_mayoral_control.

96. Macinnes has written extensively on public education. Among his works are *Wrong for All the Right Reasons: How White Liberals Have Been Undone by Race* (A Twentieth Century Fund Book published by NYU Press, 1996), and "Kids Who Pick the Wrong Parents and Other Victims of Voucher Schemes" (A Twentieth Century Fund/Century Foundation white paper, 1999).

97. http://www.takingnote.tcf.org/2010/08/four-lessons-from-new-yorks-test-results.

98. The New York Civil Liberties Union has been monitoring police abuse in the public schools for much of the Bloomberg era. The material in this section draws heavily from two sources: (1) "Criminalizing the Classroom," http://www.nyclu.org/pdfs/criminalizing_the_classroom_report.pdf; (2) The federal class action suit filed on January 20, 2010 by the NYCLU and the ACLU Foundation.

99. *New York Times* columnist Bob Herbert and many other observers have written extensively about police misconduct and abuse in the public schools. http://www.nytimes.com/2010/03/06/opinion/06herbert.

100. Again, the New York Civil Liberties Union has been at the forefront of challenging Mike's repressive tactics. The material regarding his and the NYPD's approach to this protest and the subsequent demonstration at the Republican National Convention draws on the NYCLU's reports. Mike and the NYPD would tell a different story. I've been both prosecutor and civil liberties lawyer. Although my sympathies are with the latter, I know the NYCLU is far more meticulous when it comes to reporting events such as these. I accept

the NYCLU account. Readers can judge for themselves. The full report can be found at http://www.aclu.org/FilesPDFs/nyclu_arresting_protest1.pdf.

101. http://www.nytimes.com/2003/02/16/nyregion/
threats-and-responses-overview-from-new-york-to-melbourne-cries-for-peace.

102. For a detailed account of the NYPD civil liberties abuses at the Republican National Convention, see http://www.nyclu.org/pdfs/rnc_report_083005.

103. http://www.observer.com/2011/11/nypd-blocked-press-from-protest-to-protect-them/.

104. The tactic and the ensuing perjury have nothing to do with Mike. When the United States Supreme Court ruled in 1961 that evidence obtained in violation of the constitutional protection against "unreasonable searches and seizures," can't be used in state or federal courts, police adjusted their testimony, not their tactics, and most prosecutors and judges went along with it.

105. http://www.citylimits.org/conversations/author/333/andrea-batista-schlesinger.

106. http://www.nytimes.com/2011/08/04/nyregion/
new-york-plan-will-aim-to-lift-minority-youth.

107. http://New York Times, October 6, 2011, p. A25.

108. http://www.nytimes.com/2011/11/02/nyregion/
dismal-tale-of-arrest-for-tiniest-of-crimes.

109. Michael P. Jacobson, Giuliani's probation and correction commissioner, at the 2007 meeting of the American Sociological Association.

110. In 2009, 276 cases were referred.

111. *Village Voice* reporter Graham Rayman has been tracking the story from the beginning. This is an abbreviated version taken from his reporting, See www.village-voice.com/2010-05-04/news/the-nypd-tapes-inside-bed-stuy-s-81st-precinct/8/.

112. "Mike Raps Council's Push to Nix Term Limits," Michael Saul, *NY Daily News*, November 23, 2005, www.nydailynews.com/archives/news/mike-raps-council-push-nix-term-limits-article-1.585809.

113. The names and affiliations of the letter signers can be found at http://www.citylimits.org/news/articlecfm?article_id=3628.

114. The Doe Fund rounded up a group of homeless men to sit in the front row and chant their support. Mike gave the organization more than $10 million, some of it before and some after the hearings. A Doe Fund official castigated reporters for being too cynical. It was inspiring, he said, to see homeless men taking their civic responsibilities seriously.

115. "$110K Grant Kept Rev. Al Sharpton Quiet about Mayor Bloomberg Changing Term Limits," Adam Lisberg, *Daily News*, August 15, 2010.

116. Whether the mayor personally was involved seems not to have been investigated. With the federal indictment of a couple of low-level operatives, the scandal went away.

117. Following the election, a Bloomberg campaign staffer told reporters that their polling showed a much tighter race than had been reported. The message that a double-digit Bloomberg victory was inevitable was a key piece of the strategy designed to discourage President Obama and others who might stimulate a larger turnout for Thompson. The wide discrepancy in the public and private polling numbers and the result has never been explained.

118. It is almost impossible to defeat an incumbent city council member. Of the 35 non–term-limited members elected in 2001, 34 won re-election in 2005.

119. See "Roots of 'Ballot Security': Dead Voters, Party Fears and Shadowy Tactics," *New York Times*, October 4, 2011, Tom Robbins; www.nydailynews.com/opinion/john-haggerty-case-exposes-gaping-flaws-state campaign-finance-law-article-1.968006.

120. January 5, 2010, cover story in the *Village Voice*: www.villagevoice.com/2010-01-05/news/bloomberg and-thompson- the-really-odd-couple/4/.

121. The financial services industry depends less and less on physical location. The money for the few at the top grows while the jobs shrink. That so much of the debt he has saddled us with and the policies he has pursued have been driven by the idea that the city's future is tied to Wall Street's growth seems unwise and unhealthy.

122. The story repeats itself with dreary regularity. The Savings and Loan scandals involved massive financial frauds that occurred under Bush the Elder. State politicians, who wanted the S&L's chartered in their states, rolled over for the fraudsters who bought federally insured savings deposits from brokers, paid high interest rates, gave the brokers fat commissions, and moved the cash out the door in bogus real estate transactions based on over-appraised swamp land. The insiders made a bundle and taxpayers lost hundreds of billions of dollars. Yes, of course, there was more to it than that. The mechanisms are always complicated, but greed and corruption papered over with public interest rhetoric are always at the heart of it.

123. "Bloomberg's Offshore Millions," Aram Roston (additional reporting by Azi Paybarah and Reid Pillifant), *New York Observer*, April 21, 2012, www.observer.com/2010/politics/bloombergs-offshore-millions.

124. For Barrett's full account of this and other Bloomberg conflict of interest stories, see http://www.villagevoice.com/2009-09-01/news/bloomberg-keeps-his-billions-separate-from-his-mayoral-obligations-yeah-right/.

125. "Dissecting the Claims: Exaggeration Amid Truth," Michael Barbaro, www.nytimes.com/2009/10/28/nyregion/28fact.

126. http://www.noticingnewyork.blogspot.com. White is a former state housing finance official.

127. It's only a curbstone opinion. I have neither expertise nor data to back it up,

but the notion that bad teachers are primarily responsible for our failed education system has always seemed foolish to me. My wife and I have watched a
couple of generations of Independence Plaza kids grow up in a housing complex that is integrated along class, racial, and ethnic lines. They've attended
the local schools and hung out together. We see them coming back to visit
their parents, bringing their own kids with them. They aren't rich and they
come in all colors and backgrounds and those we know seem to have turned
out very well. It leads me to wonder whether if hard budgetary choices are the
future—and they are—the monies spent to maintain the current separate and
equal (in name only) public school system might be better spent on creating
and sustaining integrated affordable housing.

128. I know this comment will anger many lawyers and other advocates. I can only
say that it's based on what I witnessed, that it isn't universally true (there were
some few cases that did work out for the tenants; these were due, I believe, to
peculiar circumstances), and that it occurred often enough to raise the issue:
We are far from finished with the privatization and deregulation program under
the current state and city governments and their likely successors.

129. "Where Have All the Fighters Gone?" http://www.democracynow.org/2005/11/3/
online_exclusive_read_ juan_gonzalez_article.

130. "Bloomberg and Thompson: The Really Odd Couple," http://www.villagevoice.
com/content/printVersion/1580214/.

131. "The Myth of *The New York Times*, in Documentary Form," http://www.truth-
dig.com/arts_culture/item/the_myth_of_the_new_york_times_in_documen-
tary_form_20110706/.

Index

CPSIA information can be obtained at www.ICGtesting.com
Printed in the USA
BVOW041107030612

291659BV00002B/2/P